FAR FROM SHORE

A Mother's Memoir of a Shark Attack

Margaret Kathrein
with Jonathan Kathrein

ISBN: 1-4392-4737-4
ISBN-13: 9781439247372
Library of Congress Control Number: 2009906409

Visit *www.booksurge.com* to order additional copies.

*For my mother, Mary,
my husband, Reed,
and for my three sons, Jonathan, Michael, and Eric
for showing me the importance of family.*

———

Table of Contents

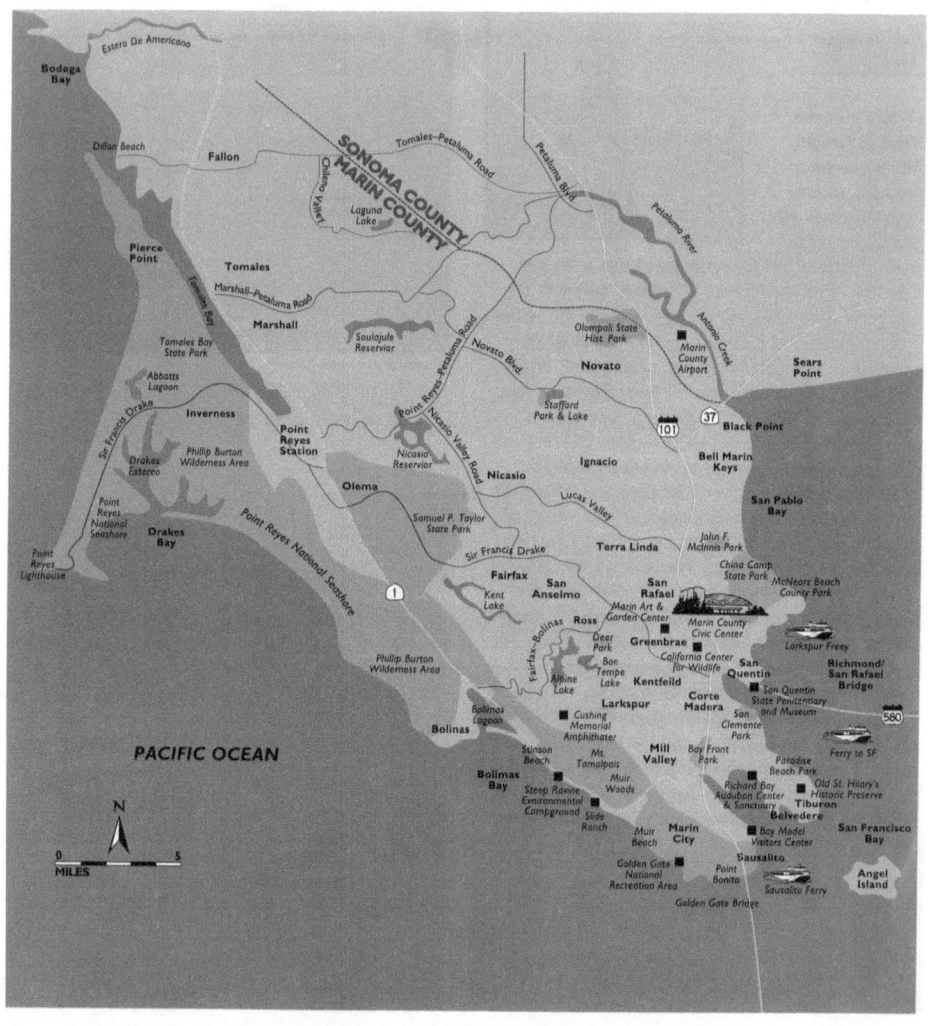

Northern California coastline, with Stinson Beach
located just north of San Francisco.

Day One

"Life is fragile and we have to treat each other well because we don't know when life will be lost."

— Jonathan Kathrein

Wednesday, August 26, 1998

8:00 A.M. – Stinson Beach, California

"LAST SHARK SIGHTING: Sunday, August 19th." The paper fluttered in the breeze at the edge of the beach. Most surfers rushed past it without noticing as they jogged to the water, boards tucked under their arms. This tattered windblown sign was hardly a convincing warning to beware of the greatest predator of the deep.

It was the morning of Wednesday, August 26th, one week after the shark warning had been posted. Stinson Beach was quiet and the small paper sign attracted little notice. The windswept sand beneath the sign showed no footprints. Like most of the surfers, my 16 year old son, Jonathan, and his friend, Sean, would not see it.

8:15 A.M. – San Francisco

I was driving Jonathan's younger brother Michael across the Golden Gate Bridge into San Francisco for his first day of high school at St. Ignatius. He'd missed the trip to the beach with his brother but that was okay, today was an important day and Michael was eager to meet new friends at Freshman Orientation.

San Francisco felt warm and strangely balmy that morning. Fog inched its way along the coast while heat settled in the inland valleys. The newspaper reported strong currents with a high surf advisory at local beaches, but I didn't have time to worry about Jonathan right now.

I didn't mind taking Michael to San Francisco. In fact I savored the extra time with him. From our home in Marin County the drive to the city took about 30 minutes. Riding in the Previa, our Toyota minivan, was a good time for the two of us to talk. I always tried to keep the communication lines open with each of my boys during these busy teenage years. As a result, I had developed a close relationship with each of them. That was something I treasured.

When we pulled up to the curb in front of school, I noticed the Pacific Ocean in the distance, obscured by fog. A throng of new students gathered outside in the chilly air.

"Take your sweatshirt, Michael," I reminded him.

"It's okay, I won't need it, Mom." He gave me a hug and disappeared into the crowd.

Michael was confident and moved easily into new situations. I was certain he'd be fine and didn't give a thought to what the day would bring. I didn't think twice about our quick goodbye. I simply turned to head home.

My husband Reed and I had chosen St. Ignatius High School or rather, Jonathan had chosen it for himself two years earlier after our friend, Debbie, had urged us to consider this well-established Jesuit school in the Sunset district of San Francisco. Jonathan loved it, and he loved seeing the ocean every day. The school had an excellent reputation and in spite of the commute, we were never sorry. Tomorrow classes would begin for all students and Michael, a freshman, would ride to school with Jonathan, now a junior.

I was relieved to be heading home and hoped the traffic wouldn't slow me down. Eric had been asleep when I'd left, and I wanted to be there to have breakfast with him. Eric, the youngest of my three sons, was at home sleeping late, enjoying his last few days of summer vacation. Next week he'd launch into sixth grade and join a new soccer team. But for today, we would spend a laid-back summer day together.

My three boys were the focus of my life, each in different ways. Jonathan, age 16, was shy and cautious, always responsible, setting the example for his younger brothers and protecting them. I could depend on him to be careful and safe. Michael, age 14, was the independent risk-taker, always pushing the limits and looking for new adventure, often with logic that was hard for me to refute. I could never anticipate his next move, but I'd come to expect him to be daring. Eric, age 10, was my affectionate little one, still young and happy to be at my side. I soaked up my closeness with each of them. Their affection was the reward that kept me going even when the family routine of sports and school became chaotic. Being a mom was my life and my joy.

Life with three boys was never dull. I loved the energy, commotion, and excitement, so different from the quiet family of my own childhood. I smiled as I thought back to the days when all three of them were in grade school together at Dixie School just two blocks from our home. I walked them to school each morning and waited for them after school. In those years we were always together.

Our boys grew up in a home filled with stories. Starting when they were little, I read all my favorite children's books to them. At night, we'd pile onto Eric's bed for bedtime stories with the lights dim. *The Hobbit,* the *Hardy Boys,* and *Boxcar Children* were their favorites. They loved the familiarity of our routine, tumbling in together, and the magical excitement of the adventures I read. Reed was always there to tuck them in. Now they were growing up and starting to explore the world on their own.

I had always tried to teach them to be good to each other. And they were, most of the time. "Brothers are best friends," I reminded them. "Brothers love each other." These were the values I hoped they'd always remember. "Other friends might come and go, but brothers are forever."

They'd taken my words to heart and I could see a special bond developing. They became inseparable friends and best buddies as they grew up together. They were a team in everything.

Reed shared my commitment to our boys and reinforced the rules I laid down. He tickled and wrestled with them on the living room floor, teasing them with his sense of humor and encouraging the family team spirit. My mother observed that in our family, "We made our own fun."

Driving home over the Golden Gate Bridge that morning, I gazed out at the Pacific Ocean. White caps tossed the big buoy just beyond the bridge and the ocean looked unsettled. I noticed the strong current flowing into the Bay. A cargo ship cutting through the waves drew my attention out to sea. But my thoughts quickly returned to the busy fall schedule that was about to kick in, with school starting tomorrow.

Just after crossing the bridge, I decided to take a quick detour to the top of the Marin Headlands for the view. I could use a moment of solitude.

At the top of the hill I pulled over and stepped out to take a look. The bay, the city of San Francisco, the bridge, and the ocean spread before me in the morning light. Although we'd lived here for almost nine years, California still seemed like an amazing new adventure and I took every opportunity to explore trails, views, and the coast. I could see Point Bonita, the thin strip of land jutting out to sea with a lighthouse at the point. A fog horn sounded its steady pitch, piercing the morning air.

I admired the view but didn't linger. Already I could see a steady line of cars creeping up the hill, snaking around the curves, jamming the road to the beach. Traffic to the coast would be heavy with everyone trying to escape the inland heat.

I thought of Jonathan and the fun he'd have at the beach with Sean, his best friend. I recalled how he'd spent the evening talking on the phone, excitedly making plans and double-checking everything for their trip to

Stinson Beach. It was his last day of summer vacation and he wanted everything to be perfect. The weather forecast for fog at the coast and high surf didn't bother him. Jonathan was a strong swimmer and loved the excitement of the waves. It would be a good day for surfing.

Now that he was sixteen he could drive to the beach on his own. Like any mother, I worried about the narrow, curvy roads and oncoming traffic, but I knew he'd be careful.

Jonathan relished the preparation almost as much as the trip to the beach. In his usual methodical fashion, he'd made lists of things to remember. He laid out his blue shortie wetsuit, his yellow Morey Mach 7-SS boogie board, his big striped beach towel, his green Nalgene water bottle, his hooded grey sweatshirt, sunscreen, snacks, and his canvas lifeguard hat, the one with the wide brim in case it was sunny.

Finally, around 10:00 pm he set his car keys next to the door along with his favorite Blue Dragon sunglasses. He saved these sunglasses for special days. Now, he was ready for the morning.

Before going to bed he had called Sean one last time. "Okay, I'll pick you up early." I smiled as I overheard him say "early" because Jonathan was known as the sleepy-head in our family. My mother often remarked that he could "sleep the clock around." But on beach days he was always eager to get an early start.

"G' night, Mom."

"Sweet dreams, Jonathan."

I gave him a kiss and tucked him in. To me, the goodnight kiss was a reminder of everything important in my life. I remembered how my mother tucked me in and made me feel safe. I'd fall asleep listening to her humming and talking to my father downstairs. I loved hearing her singing...and she was always singing or humming. It was not just the songs, but the sound of her voice, reminding me of her presence and love. I'd always felt secure. Now I wanted my boys to grow up in a strong family, just as I had.

Over the years when I was a child growing up in Wisconsin, my family celebrated each little victory. Any good news or a good report card was cause for a special dinner. Sometimes my mother baked an apple pie, or we'd walk to the neighborhood ice cream shop. I loved to try every new flavor, but my mother always ordered her favorite, buttered pecan. My father loved black walnut ice cream because it reminded him of the walnuts he'd picked as a boy on the family farm in Iowa. I'd spent many summers visiting my relatives on that farm, and I knew how important it was to have strong family connections.

My father was one of three brothers, too, and I'd noticed how he and his brothers always joked with each other and how they loved to be together. My father's love taught me a lot about families. People were most important in his life. I felt his love, although it was often unspoken. His quiet affection made me feel special and gave me the unending confidence that I could do anything, and he'd be there for me. The feeling of connection with my family was the most comforting feeling to me as a child. Although he was no longer with us, my father's continuing love was evident in my three boys; I was sure of it.

One summer, I'd taken Reed and our boys to visit Uncle Howard's farm where my father and his brothers had grown up near Tipton, Iowa. The farm, called "Harmony Point," offered many new adventures for Jonathan, Michael, and Eric - exploring old barns and riding along in the pickup truck to visit the cattle in the field. One afternoon, Jonathan decided to take a walk in the cornfield that towered well over his head and stretched as far as anyone could see. After he'd disappeared for what seemed like a very long time, everyone worried about how he might walk for acres in the wrong direction, and how he might not find his way back. Soon my cousins were calling his name, and Reed climbed a tall tree to look out over the cornfield. Finally, after anxious hours of calling and searching, Jonathan appeared, looking happy and proud. "I don't know why you were worried," he said, "I wasn't lost…just exploring." Even then, his spirit of adventure was strong.

My mother was an important role model and confidant for me in every stage of my life. She knew the meaning of determination. She'd grown up during the Great Depression, and was the first in her family to graduate from college. She practiced the piano and won music contests. When she became a music teacher, her girl's choir won a national competition. She always sent part of her paycheck home each month to help her parents on the farm in Iowa. I admired her sense of family loyalty, even while venturing out to achieve her goals.

For me, my mother set the unspoken standard. I wanted to emulate her confidence and her sense of achievement, while creating her own path. With her encouragement I'd learned to speak French, studied in Paris, and explored the world as an international flight attendant for Pan American. When I graduated from law school, my mother was there to celebrate my success. When my children were born, she was there, nurturing a close relationship with each of them as they grew, reading stories, sitting on the floor building Lego forts, teaching them to play cat's cradle and duets at the piano.

She'd protected and inspired me as a child. With her support, I always knew I could do anything. I wanted my children to feel that same confidence in themselves.

Jonathan and I were nearly inseparable from the start. He was my first child and an answer to my dreams. When he was born my life revolved around him and I wanted everything to be perfect. When he was little, he never wanted me to leave him and I gladly gave up other activities, even sleep, to spend my time with him. He'd cry every time I left him with a babysitter so I rarely did, and at night I'd sit on the edge of his bed folding laundry or reading to him, because he didn't like to be alone in the dark. He was my constant buddy, so easygoing that I found being a mother the most rewarding job in the world. I was sure Jonathan needed me and I wanted to always be there for him.

Living in Chicago before he was born, I'd established my career as a food and drug attorney in a fast-paced law firm. I loved the professional world, but my priorities were changing. While Jonathan was little, I began to scale back my law career to spend more time with him. I wanted to be home with him, to teach and nurture, just as my mother had been done for me.

When Michael was born two years later, I cut back my law practice even more to be at home more with my boys. Three years later when Eric arrived, I decided to become a full-time mom. Although in some ways it was a difficult choice, I wanted my family to come first. I put my professional life on hold and took an indefinite leave of absence from the practice of law, hoping to get back to it in a few years.

I never regretted putting my law career on hold. Instead of the law, I studied all the books I could find on parenting and raising children. I believed it was important to be with my boys during their early years and I was happy with the ever-changing routine of being a mom. Reed agreed that my being home was the most important decision we could make about raising our boys. Then, when Jonathan was in second grade, he wrote a Thanksgiving letter in his childish script, "I'm thankful for mom staying home with me, and for a good family." This was the only reward I ever needed.

Reed was the working member of our family team. His career in securities law continued to pick up speed and with his workload increasing, he worked long hours. "Someone has to be home," we agreed. I was convinced I'd made the right decision.

I became a regular volunteer in our boys' classrooms at Dixie Elementary School and I waited for them every day after school when the bell rang. One afternoon, Jonathan's second grade teacher observed, "Mrs. Kathrein, you're always so present." Her comment surprised me, but it was one of the nicest compliments I'd ever received. I'd never really thought that my being there was anything out of the ordinary. To me, being present for my children was an important part of being a family and they seemed happy to see me there each day after school.

Jonathan was the conscientious big brother who always paid attention, and watched over his little brothers. Even without my asking, he always made sure they were safe. I knew I could depend on him because he was naturally cautious and careful and shy to venture out.

Somehow everything was working smoothly, according to my dreams. We were the Leave-it-to Beaver family with happy children and few disagreements. The boys loved each other and they were the most fun, easy children I could imagine. No major challenges entered our lives. I had no experience with crisis and no reference for disaster in my life. My life and my adventures had always been safe. I didn't stop to think that life could be fragile or how easily it could all be taken from us.

Our first home was in Tower Lakes, Illinois, a rural and peaceful community on the outskirts of Chicago. We lived near cornfields, a soccer field, and a small lake. There were strong Midwest families with plenty of neighborhood kids outside playing games and riding bikes. Life was simple; we were friends with our neighbors, we shared wide lawns, we believed in our dreams, and families were everything. Growing up in the Midwest was one fun adventure after another. Our boys spent their days playing outside climbing trees, building igloos, and ice skating on the pond. Following my mother's example, I planned family outings, picnics, camping trips, and long days at the beach.

Jonathan had many connections with water, even as a young child growing up in Illinois. He loved the Tower Lakes Beach just a block from our house, and the lake was a big part of his life. While Reed was at work in the Sears Tower, we spent summer days swimming in the warm water, floating in the waves, and building castles in the sand. Michael was learning to swim too, and little Eric played in the sand. During those long days, I taught the boys to enjoy the beach, the gentle waves, the changing sky, and the soft breeze over the lake. Jonathan was always comfortable in the water and soon he was strong enough to swim across the lake.

Each day, all the neighborhood kids played a game called, "Sharks and Minnows," splashing and chasing each other in the water. "It's more fun being a minnow," Jonathan said in breathless excitement as he dried off with a beach towel, "because minnows can swim really fast to get away from the shark."

On weekends we visited my mother at her home on the shore of Lake Mendota in Madison, Wisconsin. During the two hour drive, I played "Baby Beluga" and "The Wheels on the Bus" and the boys sang along. My mother the music teacher had taught them the words to all the songs.

Grandma Mac gave the boys lots of special attention and her lakefront home offered plenty of excitement during every season. They never tired of swimming in the warm lake, trying, but not always succeeding, to fish for lake perch using hot dogs as bait, feeding the ducks, then splashing off the pier into the water and scaring them. On rainy days they'd create giant spider webs, covering her entire basement with a tangled maze of string. On summer nights we'd gaze at shooting stars above the lake from Grandma's patio and admire the lights of the state capitol reflected in the water across the lake. In the winter we'd lace up our ice skates to shovel a hockey rink or skate across the frozen lake, always racing home for hot chocolate when it got dark.

As they grew, each summer's visit to Grandma's house was another watery experience. Reed taught our boys to be confident swimmers. They were fearless, jumping into the choppy, murky lake with carefree abandon, never worrying about those long stringy weeds, the dense water, or the little silvery fish that might nibble their toes. Swimming in Lake Mendota was an adventure and they were thrilled with every splash, always within the safety of Grandma's pier and our watchful eyes. Jonathan loved the excitement of lake with its white caps on a windy day, yet he always dreamed of the ocean.

Soon that dream was realized. When Jonathan was in first grade, Reed and I decided to move our young family to California in search of new horizons. Northern California seemed like the perfect destination with its rugged coastline, endless beaches, and the outdoor adventures it would offer. We couldn't wait to explore the great wilderness that awaited us.

While we were still living in Illinois anticipating our big move, North Barrington School held a poetry contest. My mother encouraged Jonathan to write a poem about his dream. "Your poem doesn't have to rhyme," she said. "You can write free verse." In his poem, he imagined the ocean he would see:

California -
When we move to California
There won't be any snow...
But we'll have an ocean,
And it will be really warm there,
And it will be really fun there....

- by Jonathan, 1ˢᵗ grade

Jonathan won the poetry contest with his rhythmic words that resonated with the pulse of the waves. He couldn't wait to get there for his new adventures to begin.

California seemed like paradise after winters in Chicago. Northern California offered every adventure, and we were not disappointed. We explored beaches, discovered tide pools, and raced down sand dunes. The Pacific Ocean was extremely cold, the waves were wild, and we loved it.

Jonathan was eager for the challenge. He plunged into the cold water, running back to shore to warm up after each wave, while Reed stood watch on the beach. His long legs grew strong and soon he was able to swim out into the waves. His swimming skills improved with his years on our local Lucas Valley swim team. I never worried about Jonathan in the water because he was a lifeguard at the pool and a cautious, capable swimmer.

The ocean soon became a favorite part of our lives. We took weekend family trips along the coast to Stinson Beach, Muir Beach, and Monterey. At Point Reyes National Seashore we found secluded places for beachcombing, hiking, and swimming along the coast. As our boys grew older, they learned to brave the cold water. We were careful and I assumed we'd always be safe.

"The shark's primary function is to eat.
The only way they can find out if
we're edible is to take a bite."

- Ralph Collier, Shark Expert

9:00 A.M. – Lucas Valley

After delivering Michael to San Francisco, I was anxious to get home to Eric. The morning traffic eased as I passed San Rafael and approached the Lucas Valley exit.

I remembered how quiet the house had seemed earlier that morning when I'd tiptoed down the hallway to the boys' rooms. They were still asleep. Jonathan and Eric were together in a room they'd shared since we'd moved to California. Michael preferred the independence of his own room across the hall.

The morning air felt chilly and the breeze moved the leaves on the orange tree outside the open window next to Jonathan's bed. Jonathan opened his eyes and I pulled the covers over his shoulders.

"Morning mom," he whispered, gazing outside to check out the day.

"Morning Jonathan," I replied, trying not to wake Eric. I wondered if Jonathan might go back to sleep, but a minute later he was on his feet. He threw on a t-shirt and headed down the hall to the kitchen.

"Today's the last beach day for the summer," he reminded me.

"Yes, I can tell you can't wait to get out there."

"Let's have breakfast, Mom."

I was happy to be included in his morning plans. I followed him into the kitchen where he grabbed a bowl and the box of Grape Nuts, his favorite cereal. I sat down with my cup of tea. While we were sitting at the breakfast table, our neighbor Ken stuck his head in the kitchen door to say hello.

"Hi guys, what's for breakfast" he asked with a grin. He often stopped by if our door was open, just to say hi or to shoot baskets with the boys when they were outside

Ken was a good friend, one of the first neighbors we'd met after moving to California from Chicago. I felt I'd known him all my life. He was a Midwesterner. He'd moved with his family from Chicago and his son, Alan, was Eric's buddy. With our common backgrounds, our families had grown in friendship over the years.

"I haven't seen you guys since you came back from your vacation. How was Maine? " he asked.

"Great, we spent a lot of time in the water," I replied. "Do you have time for coffee?"

"No, I have to get to work before the traffic gets any worse. Thanks anyway. Hey, Jonathan, you start school tomorrow... I guess you'd better have some fun today."

"I'm going to the beach," Jonathan replied.

"Well, don't have too much fun."

Ken's familiar chuckle echoed as he headed out the door.

After breakfast, I'd overheard Jonathan call the lifeguard tower at Stinson Beach to confirm the latest conditions. "How's the surf today?" he asked. I didn't hear their reply, but I heard Jonathan say, "....Okay... good.... we're heading out."

"Okay, Mom, I'm off to pick up Sean in Mill Valley," he said, as he grabbed his sunglasses and the keys he'd set by the door the night before. While he gathered up his gear getting ready to leave for Stinson, I was getting ready to take Michael to school.

"Please be careful on those curvy roads," I said in my worried mother tone of voice, thinking of the winding roads to the coast.

"Yes, of course. Don't worry, Mom. I'm the most careful driver you know."

I could tell he was eager to get going, but leaving seemed to take forever and I hated to see him go off on his own. I tried not to think too much about it, but I knew he was lingering.

He'd just turned sixteen and he seemed to share some of my separation anxiety. Now that he was a teenager, letting go wasn't easy for me and at times it wasn't easy for him either. We'd spent so much time together over the years, our lives were strongly connected.

Finally he seemed ready to go. I wanted to give him a hug and wave goodbye as I always did whenever my boys left home.

"Bye, Mom," he said as he gave me a quick hug and headed toward the door.

"Bye, Jonnyboy." I brushed a kiss onto his cheek as he hurried past. He disappeared out the door. Then, for some reason, he came back in.

"I almost forgot my sandals," he said, sliding his suntanned feet into his flip flops. "See you tonight," he said as the kitchen door slammed behind him. Then, to my surprise, he stuck his head in again.

"Bye, Mom, I love you."

"Bye, Jonathan, I love you too."

I noticed his hesitation and followed him out the door. The next thing I knew, I was standing beside his car, savoring this long goodbye. I'll never forget how apprehensive I felt as we lingered in the driveway, but I refused to let it bother me. I didn't believe in premonitions and it would be foolish, I thought, to make a big deal of this.

"Please don't be late for dinner...."

"I'll be careful...don't worry, Mom." By now he'd noticed the furrow in my brow. He gave me one last hug trying to ease my concern and climbed into his car.

I waved as he backed out of the driveway and turned onto the street. "I'll see you soon," he called from his car window.

I watched until he disappeared. For some reason, I didn't want to turn my back.

Now, as I was returning home from San Francisco, I thought of Jonathan and Sean. They were probably nearing the beach, perhaps passing the faded green sign we'd seen so many times along the way, "Stinson Beach - Population 486, Elevation 26."

Even with its popular beach, the town of Stinson had managed to keep its quaint, small-town feel with only one surf shop, a few small cafes, a good little book store, and a few art galleries, but not a single gas station. On a busy weekend the town overflowed with locals, artists, fishermen, ranchers, cyclists, surfers, and tourists. Yet somehow it remained undisturbed. Little had changed here over the years. Stinson still looked like it must have forty years ago.

A few years earlier, Jonathan had chosen sharks as the topic for his sixth grade term paper. He'd described the white shark as an important predator in the marine ecosystem of the California coast. He'd learned that the white shark was a protected species in California. Seals were protected too and, as a result of that protection, their population had increased, providing ample food for sharks along the Pacific Coast.

"Seals are the favorite food of the white shark," he'd written. "A surfer in a wetsuit looks like the dark silhouette of a seal from the shark's perspective, looking up from below against the bright surface of the water."

His report concluded with a personal observation, "Each year, human-shark interactions increase, with more people entering the water for recreation. But I've never seen a shark, or heard of anyone seeing one along the coast where I live."

1:00 P.M.

Eric and I were at home that afternoon in Lucas Valley, our quiet neighborhood 12 miles north of the Golden Gate Bridge. Our valley was just beyond the fog that often blanketed the city in the summer months. The scent of jasmine floated through the open door near my desk, from the trellis loaded with blossoms just outside the kitchen. Our backyard was sunny and the afternoon air was still, almost eerily so. An unforgiving August sun reflected off our well-worn fence with such intensity it hurt my eyes. Lucas Valley sweltered in the August heat.

I noticed a photo in the morning newspaper of a surfer carving down the face of a big wave. The caption read, "High surf advisory and foggy conditions expected to continue at the coast." Nothing new for August, I thought to myself. Even so, I felt anxious with Jonathan out at the beach so far from home. I knew he wouldn't take chances in the water, but I'd be relieved when he returned after the long drive.

I knew that even on hot summer days, the beach could be cold and windy. I'd seen the fog hovering at the coast earlier that morning when I'd crossed the Golden Gate Bridge. I was glad Jonathan had packed extra clothes. Any day at Stinson could be unpredictable.

I could hear the voices and laughter of children playing at the Dixie soccer field down the street from our house. It was the comforting, familiar sound of home. Just two days earlier we'd returned from vacation with our friends, the Brennan family, at their cabin on Mousam Lake in Maine. Our kids had spent every day swimming and waterskiing. They could never get enough of the water, I thought.

That afternoon, Eric and I played baseball in the backyard. "I think I need the practice more than you do," I laughed as I tried to pitch the balls and he practiced his swing. He managed to hit a few good ones, even though I wasn't much of a pitcher.

"Higher, Mom," he said. "You're pitching too low."

"Okay, I'll try. There, how's that?"

"That's better, Mom," he replied, as he hit the next one over the fence.

Reed had left early that morning, expecting a busy day at his law office in the Financial District of San Francisco. Michael had arranged a ride home from school with his friend, Ian, who lived nearby. He'd planned to stay there until I picked him up later that afternoon.

2:30 P.M.

"Mom, it's so hot today, I wish we'd gone to the beach with Jonathan. I'd like to swim in that cold ocean," Eric said.

"Yes, that sounds like fun. I'll take you to the beach this weekend if you'd like." He was only eleven and I couldn't let him go to go to the beach without me.

"Okay," he replied happily, looking forward to a weekend outing. "I'm sure Michael and Jonathan will want to go with us. And Dad, too."

I thought of Jonathan kicking out through the waves to ride the surf. I hoped he wasn't cold. His wetsuit was getting too small for his long legs. I recalled the day the boys had found it at a neighborhood garage sale. It had short sleeves and short legs and it was not as thick as the full body wetsuits most of the surfers wore, but it helped keep him warm in the cold water. The wetsuit had lasted longer than we expected, but we'd need to get him a new one soon.

A good wetsuit can make a big difference in the cold water of Northern California. Most surfers wear full body 4/3 neoprene wetsuits with a chest thickness of 4 millimeters and 3 millimeters in the arms and legs. Some surfers even wear booties and hoods so they can stay out in the cold water longer. Wetsuits fill with water that creates a thin layer of insulation between the skin and the suit. Just as a person's body warms the air inside a sweatshirt, the surfer's body warms the layer of water inside the suit, making it an insulating barrier against the cold. With his arms and legs exposed, Jonathan would feel the cold, but the wetsuit allowed him to stay in the water a little longer.

3:30 P.M.

The ringing telephone shattered the stillness of the summer afternoon. I resented the disturbance and at first I didn't move.

Eric ran to grab the phone, eager to know if one of his friends might be calling.

"Hello. Eric speaking," he answered politely.

Then I heard a long pause. He listened without saying a word. I could tell he didn't recognize the voice on the phone. His face looked puzzled.

"Yes, she's here. Just a minute, please."

"Here Mom...It's for you," he said. "I think someone is trying to sell you something." He handed the phone to me without further explanation.

"Hello?" I answered. I was impatient, offended by the interruption, not knowing what to expect.

"Is this Mrs. Kathrein?"

I paused for a moment. At first I didn't reply.

"Do you have a son named Jonathan?" the voice on the phone asked.

"Yes...I do....Why?"

My voice trailed off in anticipation of the next words. This was not an ordinary call. Already I was a different person, caught up in what was to come.

"My name is Beth," the voice on the phone continued. "I'm a social worker for the Trauma Center at John Muir Hospital in Walnut Creek." She paused. I held my breath.

"Jonathan's been in a slight accident."

The words were spoken calmly, yet difficult for me to comprehend. Seldom had words seemed more harsh. I tried to answer. I couldn't find my voice. I was too stunned to speak. Finally, I took a deep breath.

"What...Jonathan....in an accident?"

A vivid scene flashed into my mind. I pictured Jonathan's car on the road to Stinson Beach with broken glass scattered on the pavement. Somber trees obscured the light. I was sure it must be something minor. Jonathan would be okay, I told myself. He was a careful driver. Surely he could not be seriously hurt.

I inhaled, forcing myself back to the present, still not knowing what to say.

"Jonathan was attacked by a shark at Stinson Beach..." she said.

With these words, a chill swept over me. Suddenly everything shifted. This news took my breath away. I was too shocked and horrified to speak. I felt weak. My knees crumbled and I sank into the chair beside my desk. Everything stood still. I stared at the phone blankly. This was something I couldn't comprehend. I tried to speak but no words would come. My heart pounded. I started to tremble.

"What did you say?" I fought back tears as I endured what seemed like a deadly silence, waiting to hear the next words.

"A shark attacked your son in the water at Stinson Beach." She repeated the message clearly and distinctly.

I struggled to find words. "A shark? At Stinson Beach? Not Jonathan." Disbelief resonated in my voice.

Eric heard the panic in my voice. He took my hand, trying to understand what was happening.

I held my breath, waiting to hear the rest. Finally, after what seemed like forever, I managed to speak. Questions tumbled out of my confusion.

"What happened? Is he alive?"

"The shark damaged his leg and hip but I don't know how severe the injuries are. He was brought here by helicopter. The doctors are evaluating his condition right now."

This was the call every mother dreads. A shark attack was something I'd never even dreamed of. None of this made any sense. Jonathan was in trouble and he was so far away.

"The doctors are working to stabilize him, to stop the bleeding, and evaluate his condition. I'm afraid he's in a great deal of pain."

I listened without speaking. In one stroke, all plans were out the window and everything had changed.

"Mrs. Kathrein, the doctors would like to take your son into surgery before you arrive at the hospital. Do we have your permission?"

She waited for my reply. I couldn't find my voice. I knew this was done only in serious cases where immediate surgery was necessary to save a life. Finally, I stuttered, "Yes, if that's what you need to do."

"The doctors will take him into surgery immediately."

She kept the information brief. I hung on every word.

"Mrs. Kathrein, the doctors want you to come to the hospital right away."

"Yes…okay…"

"I think it might be best for you to take the back roads. There will be a lot of traffic at this time of day." Her kind voice sounded reassuring, but the message was simply unthinkable.

"When you get here, please use the Emergency Room entrance."

"I can try to get Jonathan on the phone if you'd like," she went on. "Would you like to speak to your son before he goes into surgery?"

"Yes, please," I said.

"I'll try to take the portable phone into the Emergency Room. Things might be a little noisy in there. Please hold on for a moment…." I waited through another terrible silence…. Minutes passed. I could hear an indistinguishable clamor in the background.

Finally I heard the familiar sound I wanted to hear.

"Mom....?" I was flooded with gratitude at the sound of his voice. As if a lost child was now found.

"Jonathan? Oh my goodness...Are you all right?" I took a deep breath and waited for him to continue.

"Mom...I'm okay, Mom...but my leg really hurts."

I started to tremble, trying to picture what he was enduring so far away. Jonathan's steady voice amazed me. He wasn't crying or hysterical. And yet I wondered how he could handle something so terrifying and painful. I detected a melancholy in the tone his voice, as if a dream had been shattered.

"Mom...I don't know how bad it is."

"I'll be there as soon as I can. I'm on my way. I love you, Jonathan." I tried to sound brave, but I didn't feel brave at all. I was terrified. I had to get there. To be with him. I didn't want him to face this uncertainty and the pain all alone. It would be a lot for anyone, and he was so young.

"I love you, Mom." His voice faded away abruptly and I heard no further sound.

Eric squeezed my hand, bringing my thoughts back to the present.

"Mom? What's wrong, Mom?"

"It's Jonathan," I said, hardly breathing, "Jonathan's been attacked by a shark."

"What? A shark? Attacked Jonathan?"

Eric looked up at me, bewildered. His eyes reflected my own panic. We hugged each other tightly, trying to comfort each other.

"Don't worry, Eric. He's going to be okay. Jonathan's a strong big brother," I said, hoping to reassure Eric as well as myself. My voice wavered as I tried to diminish the horrible possibilities. Somehow we both remained unconvinced. I realized how scary all of this must sound to an eleven year old. It was just as scary for me. A shark attack didn't happen in anyone's ordinary life.

Okay, I reminded myself, I'm the mom, and I need to be the solid one. And yet, dreadful thoughts kept creeping back into my mind. Somehow, I had to maintain my composure. The alternative was to scream with disbelief that this could happen to my son. What if Jonathan didn't make it? My emotions were screaming inside of me. I thought of the voice on the phone and wondered if she'd told me everything.

"Eric, we need to call Dad and tell him what happened so he can get to the hospital too."

I gathered my composure long enough to call Reed. I dialed the direct number for his office and heard his phone ringing. I wondered what to say as I heard him finally come on the line.

"Reed? You'd better sit down." My voice was cracking. I couldn't hide the tears welling in my throat. I couldn't think of the right words.

"Marge....what's wrong?"

At the sound of Reed's soft voice I simply blurted it out. "Jonathan's been attacked by a shark at the beach."

"What? Are you kidding?"

"No. It's true. The hospital just called. They're taking him into surgery right away."

"Is he okay? What hospital?" I could tell Reed was already moving toward the door.

"He's at John Muir Trauma Center in Walnut Creek. I don't know how to get there. But I do know Jonathan is waiting for us."

"Okay," he said, "I'm heading to the hospital right now. I'll meet you there."

Next I called Michael. By now, he'd returned from San Francisco to the home of his friend Ian, not far from ours. Ian's dad was a counselor at St. Ignatius and had given both boys a ride home to Lucas Valley after orientation.

"Michael?"

"Hi Mom," he said happily.

"Michael....Jonathan's been attacked by a shark at the beach. We have to get to the hospital. I'll pick you up right away."

"What was a shark doing at the beach?" Michael asked in disbelief. "Don't sharks live out in deep water?" He was as stunned and confused as I was.

"Michael, I don't know." I could not explain and I couldn't think. "I'll pick you up right away. You can help me find the way to the hospital."

I hung up the phone and turned to Eric. "Let's hurry. I need you to help me be strong."

"Okay, Mom. C'mon." He proudly rose to the occasion, wanting to help.

I had no idea what to expect and no time to think. I found my keys and grabbed my purse before we rushed out the door. Was this what being a mother meant? I had to be prepared for anything. Even a shark attack? Okay, I can do this. Within five minutes we were out the door.

Horrible images raced through my head. I pictured Jonathan...alone on the beach, injured and unable to move, surrounded by strangers. I wasn't there when it happened, but I should have been. I felt I'd failed my job as a mother when he needed me most. I thought of everything I could have done differently. Most of all I should have been there when he was hurt and alone. I was filled with regret.

I remembered the day Eric collided with a fifth grade friend on the soccer field at school. Within minutes I arrived to console him and take him to the Emergency Room where the doctor gave him fourteen stitches. I was there for him, as a mom should be when a child is hurt. But now we were so far away from Jonathan.

4:00 P.M.

Michael was ready to go and waiting outside when Eric and I arrived at Ian's house. He was already studying the map.

"I see Walnut Creek...it's way over there," he said.

"Good, you'll be my navigator because I don't know the way."

"I can help you find it, Mom" Michael said with certainty.

"Thank goodness we're together on this journey."

We started out for the hospital, still an hour's drive away in what was quickly becoming rush hour traffic. We hardly spoke during the drive. I prayed Jonathan would be okay.

"Authorities have closed Stinson
Beach until further Notice."

\- KGO Radio News

4:15 P.M.

The media picked up the story even before we reached the hospital. I heard the news flash break into the regular programming on my car radio. The "breaking news" caught my attention and I heard the announcer report the headline story.

"We have breaking news from Stinson Beach where a sixteen-year-old Bay Area boy was attacked by a shark." I gasped. "The youth was airlifted to John Muir Trauma Center where he remains in critical condition. We are awaiting further details about his condition and we will continue to update this story as more information becomes available."

"Oh my gosh, Mom," said Eric. "They're talking about Jonathan."

I didn't want to cry, but the tears rolled down my face. The report was chilling, and all too real.

"Mom," Michael said, "You have to pull over if you're going to cry. You can't drive with tears in your eyes."

"Yes, I know," I said, taking a breath, trying to hold back the tears. "But we need to get to Jonathan."

"Mom...Are you okay? Don't worry, Mom. You're doing great," Eric said.

"I'm okay. I just want to get there."

"Okay, let's try to keep going," Michael replied. "You can do it. Jonathan's waiting for us."

My sons were speaking to me with conviction, offering guidance and support, just as I'd always given them. The roles were reversed but the lessons were clear – they were trying to reassure me and I had to be strong. The firmness in their young voices helped me regain my composure. I smiled to reassure Michael and Eric that I was all right. Inside I was frantic to know if Jonathan was all right too.

Radio reports of the shark attack were repeated every few minutes while we drove across the Richmond Bridge…heading to the East Bay… past miles of unfamiliar landscape…closer to the hospital…not knowing. "Details are still sketchy," they said, "but surfers confirm that someone was attacked by a shark at Stinson Beach this afternoon. One surfer here on the beach tells us what he saw…."

"I was in the water when I heard someone calling for help and trying to swim to shore… wow, I was right there…wow, that could have been me. Then I saw a lifeguard pulling him onto the beach… he was bleeding pretty bad…."

"The name of the victim is being withheld, pending news of his condition," the announcer said. Already, news of the shark attack was spreading quickly and we hadn't reached the hospital yet.

"It's like the stories you always hear and you wonder who it is," Michael said. "But this time we know who it is."

4:45 P.M.
Trauma Center at John Muir Hospital, Walnut Creek, California

We arrived at the hospital in the heat of the late afternoon, silently wondering how he would be, not knowing what to expect. My mind drifted. I was numb with anxiety, thinking only of Jonathan. The hospital looked white and pale against the surrounding golden hills. Large windows reflected the late afternoon sun.

I followed the signs to the Emergency Entrance. I didn't see a helicopter landing pad, but I knew it must be somewhere on the roof, out of sight. The parking lot near the Emergency Room was filled with black SUVs and vans. Michael was quick to size up the situation. "Mom, these are all television SUV's and trucks." Only then did I notice reporters, cameras, sound booms, satellite dishes, and antennas everywhere.

"What's going on?" Eric asked.

"I guess they're here because of Jonathan..." I replied.

We found a spot to park, away from the center of activity, hoping the reporters might not notice us. But when Michael, Eric and I started walking quickly toward the Emergency Room door, they spotted us immediately. Four or five reporters holding microphones hurried over to us, and behind them more people with cameras. I was too worried and distracted to gather my thoughts.

I recognized the blonde woman I'd seen on the Channel 5 news. "Are you the family of the shark victim?" she asked.

The word "victim" sounded so harsh. I dreaded the thought of Jonathan as a "victim."

Then suddenly questions came from everywhere.

"...Is your son the one who was attacked?"

"Do you have any information about his condition?"

"...Do you know how it happened?"

"I'm Rebecca Sanders of local CBS, so sorry to disturb you at a time like this...but...was your son attacked by the shark at Stinson Beach?" She pushed forward in front of the men, wanting to connect woman to woman.

"Yes, he's my son."

"I'm a mom too...I know how you must feel. Can you tell me...what happened to your son?"

"Do you know anything about his injuries?" Other voices interrupted....

"Have you talked to him?"

"Yes," I answered. I spoke to him for only a minute on the phone before we left home."

"What did he say?"

"He said, 'I'm okay Mom, but my leg really hurts.' He sounded brave, but I could tell he was in a lot of pain. He couldn't really talk."

"What's his condition now?"

"The doctors have taken him into surgery. That's all we know."

One of the reporters turned to Michael. "I'm sure you've been to the beach with your brother... Was he ever afraid of sharks at Stinson Beach?"

"My brother never worried about sharks at the beach," Michael replied. "We grew up in the Midwest, swimming in lakes. We never thought about sharks in the water." Hearing Michael's confidence, the reporters crowded closer.

"Did your brother know about the Red Triangle...had he heard about any recent shark sightings...did he try to fight back?" The throng of reporters now directed their questions to Michael. "Do you think he ever expected a shark at Stinson Beach?"

"Jonathan never worried about sharks...he's a good swimmer...he thought he was safe....shark attacks are rare, and Stinson's one of the safest places...Stinson's never had a shark attack...until today."

"What do you think about people surfing and swimming at Stinson Beach now?"

"Well...I guess we know the shark's still out there..."

We turned toward the Emergency Room. "We need to get inside to see Jonathan," I said. Their questions faded as we pushed slowly through the crowd. The entrance was marked with big red letters. My legs were shaking and I could feel the heat of the pale August sun radiating off the pavement, but I was frozen with fear.

> *"One thing we know for sure...*
> *— the shark is still out there."*
>
> **- Michael Kathrein**

5:00 P.M.

Huge automatic doors swept open as we approached the Emergency Room. Inside, the hospital was cool. The white lights seemed harsh in contrast to the yellow sunlight outside. Shiny sterile floors led down an endless corridor. The hospital seemed vacant and eerie.

Over the years, I'd taken my boys to the emergency room only for small cuts and ear infections. This time, a nightmare was unfolding in an unreal world and somewhere in it all, I would find Jonathan.

"Why is it so empty?" Michael asked.

"That's the way hospitals are," I replied.

Reed met us inside, thank goodness, and we hugged in one of those long tight hugs when you never want to let go.

"How's Jonathan?" I asked nervously.

"Haven't seen him yet....I raced to get here, but they'd already taken him into surgery," he said, still holding my hand.

"I won't get to see him?" My voice cracked.

"He's been in surgery for over an hour. We just have to wait, that's all we can do."

Just then a doctor appeared. "I'm Dr. Wong, head of the Trauma Team," he said. He was a small man, very businesslike, who seemed to have his mind on many things. "We have a team of specialists – the best in their fields – working on your son right now and I guess you could say I'm the conductor of the orchestra. It's a complex repair. We don't know how long the surgery will take or what the outcome will be. Jonathan's injuries appear to be more severe than we'd anticipated. We'll tell you more as we continue to evaluate his condition."

"Oh no..." I felt weak. I was always the strong one, but right then I started to lose it. I buried my face in Reed's shoulder. I didn't want Eric and Michael to see my tears.

"C'mon, Marge," Reed said firmly. "You're the glue that keeps us together. We all need you now. You're the strong one."

"Okay, I'll try." Inside, I felt the glue was coming apart. I needed to know what was going on with my son.

5:15 P.M.

"It's going to be a while before you can see him," said the woman at the reception desk. "I can show you where to wait, if you'd like."

"Okay...thank you," I said, looking at the empty hallways. By then, I was in shock, wishing we could be somewhere, anywhere but here on this summer day. A few hours ago everyone was fine and now we were told to wait for news of our son. I could hardly bear it.

She led us to a small room with a sofa and a few upholstered chairs arranged in a way that tried to look comforting. The sign on the door said Family Waiting Room - even the name gave me chills. I didn't want to sit or wait. I couldn't focus on anything but thoughts of Jonathan.

A large tropical fish tank dominated the room, the irony a cruel joke. "This isn't fair, that we have to wait in the fish tank room," Michael said. But we had no choice.

For a long time, Michael and Eric watched the moving ocean scene before us. One fish, larger than the others, circled just below the surface of the water, providing a grim reminder of their brother's assailant.

"I had my secretary cancel everything and rushed out the door," Reed said. "Somehow a producer from ABC found my number and called my cell phone from New York while I was crossing the Bay Bridge," he said. "I don't know how they tracked me down so quickly. The press is all over this story already."

"Really?" I said in disbelief. "It's already national news and we don't even know what's happening to Jonathan?"

"They want him on television," Reed said. "I told them we'd have to see."

"Oh, Reed I'm so glad you're here," I said. "I need your help to figure out what to do." I looked at him and knew he'd remain calm and supportive. He was solid, I felt weak. Life had suddenly changed.

5:30 P.M.

They were the only other people in the waiting room. "I'm Georgia and this is my husband, David," she said softly. "Your son must be the one who just arrived by helicopter... I know how frightened you must be."

"Yes…" I was so worried I could hardly speak, and I didn't know what to say to her. I didn't even know why she was there. But I appreciated her presence and concern.

"Don't worry," she said, "I think you son's going to be okay." She put her arm around me, offering her support, even though we'd just met. While our husbands, Reed and David, talked business, Georgia and I enfolded each other in hugs. Her faith and confidence encouraged me. I couldn't have asked for a greater gift at that moment.

5:45 P.M.

A dark haired young woman stepped into the waiting room. "Hello, my name is Tammy. I'm the hospital Public Relations Director. I'll be taking all phone requests to speak with you and your son." She held out a handful of phone messages. "We've received quite a few already," she said. "Most are reporters requesting interviews with Jonathan and all of you. I'll stay with you tonight for as long as you need me," she said.

I had not anticipated so much attention from the press, even before Jonathan was out of surgery. Their eagerness for the details surprised me while we were still uncertain of Jonathan's condition.

Tammy was not flustered by the phone calls or the throng of reporters waiting outside. She showed us a press release she'd drafted and asked us to approve the wording. As soon as we'd nodded in agreement, she issued the statement to the press:

> *"The sixteen year old shark attack victim is in critical condition at John Muir Medical Center where he remains in surgery at this time with extensive injuries to the muscles and tendons of his hip, thigh, and knee. The family is awaiting word from the doctors on the condition of their son. The extent of recovery is not yet known. No further information is being released at this time."*

The news release was on the air within minutes, she told us. Radio stations and newspapers were already spreading the story. Evening newspapers were hitting the stands with headline news of the shark attack, but we were inside worrying about Jonathan.

6:00 P.M.

An hour passed without any word from the doctors.

"Reed," I said, breaking the silence. "How much longer do you think we'll have to wait?"

"I wish I knew," was his only response.

I watched anxiously each time the elevator doors opened, hoping for some word of the surgery upstairs. Finally, a young woman dressed in green hospital scrubs approached us.

"I'm Jenan, the nurse assisting your son's surgery. I saw him when he arrived. You have a very brave son... the doctors are doing their best...and he's doing okay," she said. "That's all I know right now." I could see her eyes glistening above her surgical mask and I wondered if they were tears.

"A teenager has a close encounter
as a day of fun turns into a terrifying experience."
- Terri Merryman, KCAL 9 News

6:15 P.M.

I searched for a pay phone and deposited enough coins for a call to Wisconsin. I needed to tell my mother about Jonathan. Even more than that, I needed to hear her voice. I was reconnecting with home and my family, as had been my habit ever since my days in college.

"Mother, I have something to tell you," I began the moment she answered, not knowing where to start. "I'm at the hospital....waiting for

Jonathan..." I was barely able to control my quavering voice. I had to pause to fight back tears and collect myself. I didn't want my mother to hear how worried I really was. After a couple of deep breaths, I managed to continue. "Jonathan was attacked by a shark at the beach."

"Oh, Margie..." She instinctively called me by my childhood nickname, without realizing it, now that things were tense. "Margie..." she hadn't called me that for a long time, since I was a little girl. "How did this ever happen," she asked, trying to comprehend a shark attack

"I really don't know...."

"But, is he okay....?"

"I haven't seen Jonathan yet...and we're still waiting for the doctors...."

She was completely stunned by this news, like the rest of us. A shark attack was unheard of, especially in Wisconsin, far from the ocean, where things like this just don't happen.

"There's not much I can tell you, but I wanted you to be prepared."

"Oh my goodness. I'm so sorry . Poor Jonathan." She was the most tender, sympathetic person I knew whenever someone was hurt. She'd been alone since my father died a few years earlier, and I hated for her to be so far away from us at a time like this.

"Mother, I'll call you back as soon as I know anything more. In the meantime, please say some prayers for Jonathan. Your prayers will help more than anything."

"Yes, of course. I'll storm heaven," she replied.

Storming Heaven meant something was really important. I knew she'd say special prayers for us. And whenever Grandma Mac prayed, we had faith that things would work out.

"I have my rosary in my hand already," she said.

"Thanks, Mother. It's really urgent," I said. "We all know your prayers never go unanswered."

"Praying is something I can do. I'll put Jonathan at the top of my prayer list."

I felt better having spoken with her. She was my rock and my touchstone. I wished my own faith were as strong as my mother's. Her voice reminded me of the comfort and reassurance I'd always known as a child.

Eric, Michael, and Reed looked to me for reassurance when I returned to the waiting room. "Grandma's saying some special prayers for Jonathan," I said.

"We know Grandma has a direct line to heaven," Eric said. I think even I smiled at his confidence in her faith.

6:30 P.M.

"Let's find the gift shop and get something special for Jonathan," I suggested, trying to help Michael and Eric pass the time. Together we walked down a long hallway to the open doorway to the tiny store.

Michael spotted a stuffed shark on the shelf. "We could buy this," he said. "But it wouldn't be very funny right now."

"You're right, a shark would be too scary…Let's get this one," Eric said, holding up the cutest, softest teddy bear with a big bow tie.

"Okay, this will be our gift for Jonathan," I agreed. In truth I think I wanted this fuzzy bear to comfort all of us. Eric carried the teddy bear with him for the rest of the evening.

"I'm really hungry, Mom," Michael said.

"Okay. Let's find you something to eat."

We followed a long hallway to the hospital cafeteria, but it was closed. We bought sandwiches from a machine, but I couldn't think of eating. For me there was nothing to do but wait.

Then the words of my mother, often spoken when I was a child, came back to me. "Pray for strength," she always said, "And take it as it comes, one step at a time."

7:00 P.M.

Evening moved into night. We walked about aimlessly. At the far end of the corridor I saw someone walking toward me. The silhouette was unmistakable. Ken, our friend and neighbor, had shown up unexpectedly. I was surprised and grateful to see him. His gentle presence reminded me of a teddy bear. He was a Midwesterner with a big heart. He believed in showing up when something happened to his friends.

"You don't wait to ask questions, you come," he said giving me a hug, his soft beard brushing my cheek. "I came to check on you."

"How did you know we were here?" I asked.

"I saw you on the 5 o'clock news when you arrived at the hospital. Jonathan's shark attack is on every channel. When I heard the story, I had to come. I thought Reed might be out of town and I didn't want you to be alone."

He'd grown up with a strong sense of tradition. Families and friends support each other. I'd seen it in my own family in Wisconsin. When someone needed help, all the neighbors came. A comforting presence, my mother called it. Just having company is important when things are tough, she'd say, and now I knew it was true.

"Thanks for coming, Ken."

"Maybe you should have brought cribbage or Yatzee," Michael said. Ken always liked to play games with the boys.

"We could have a game and I'd beat you," he replied with a chuckle.

"I don't think so," Michael smiled.

"Well, we'll see next time. For now, I'll just stay."

*"Terror in the waters of the Red
Triangle Near San Francisco"*

\- Oakland Tribune

8:00 P.M.

Around eight o'clock a trim gentleman with graying temples stepped out of the elevator, wearing green surgical scrubs from head to foot. He looked energetic and alert.

"Hello, you must be Jonathan's parents. I'm Dr. Davis, one of the surgeons working on this team. We think your son is going to live...."

Our silence was profound. The message was beyond any words I'd ever experienced. I saw the look on Michael's face. I knew exactly what he was thinking. Until then, we hadn't really known that Jonathan's life was in question.

"What? You mean I might lose my brother? You're not sure if he's gonna live??"

"So far, he's a very lucky boy," Dr. Davis continued. "The shark's teeth came within one centimeter of his femoral artery. That's a thin line between survival and death. The jaws clamped down on both sides of the main artery in his leg. It was this close." He held up his little finger. "One centimeter and your son would have bled to death before ever reaching the shore."

With this news I could hardly breathe. My son's life had been reduced to clinical terms, within a centimeter from death.

"The shark severed all the major muscles and tendons in Jonathan's right thigh and damaged the tendons in his knee. The shark chipped his femur with the pressure of its jaws and the bone was exposed through the gashes in his leg. That shark made one devastating hit," the doctor continued.

"Your son lost a lot of blood. He came within minutes of needing a blood transfusion when he arrived at the hospital, but a transfusion is something I hesitate to do with any young person because of the risks. He'd have to be down to his last drop of blood, and he came pretty close."

Dr. Davis was precise, calm, and clinical. His grey hair and his professional demeanor told me he'd had years of experience. He was the expert we needed right now, but he did not give any reassurance as to the outcome.

"Will you be able to save his leg?" Reed asked.

"We have a team of specialists working on him right now. We still don't know. I need to get back to surgery now," Dr. Davis said. "I'll talk to you after we finish." Then he turned on his heel and disappeared back down the hall.

We wanted to know more, but this was not the time to ask questions. "Maybe he didn't want to give us too much information," Reed said. "Or maybe he wasn't certain of the outcome."

8:15 P.M.

Tammy, the John Muir Hospital Public Relations Director, stepped into the waiting room once again. "Reporters from the local newspapers and TV stations are still waiting outside," she said. "They want a photo of Jonathan."

Immediately my mind jumped to photos I'd seen in newspapers over the years. I remembered what it was like to see that photo and sympathize with the family, feeling grateful that my own family was safe. Now I was that mother, and we'd become that story for everyone else.

"How can I give them a photo when I don't even know if he'll be okay? What kind of photo should I give?" I didn't want it to look like a funeral picture.

"Anything you like. They promise to make copies and bring it right back."

"Well, okay," I finally agreed to give them one I carried in my wallet, a sports photo of Jonathan looking strong and vibrant in his St. Ignatius Soccer uniform.

Tammy delivered the photo to the reporters outside and, as promised, returned it a few minutes later after copies had been distributed to the press.

"You'll see Jonathan's picture on TV and in all the morning papers tomorrow," she said.

8:30 P.M.

A security guard dressed in a blue uniform approached us. "I want to warn you...the press is waiting outside for you. If you step outside that front door...they'll swarm you....They know what you're wearing."

He paused, and then continued with extreme seriousness, "If you need to go out to your car, use the back door." He pointed to a heavy gray metal door marked, *"Physicians Only."* It was a door we would otherwise never have dared to open. "I'll tell you the security code for that door...." He said, whispering the code, then disappearing to continue his rounds.

Michael and Eric started to giggle. "They know what we're wearing," Michael repeated. "It's as if we're being guarded by the Secret Service. We must be pretty important." In spite of our tension, we all laughed.

"Now we know the security code for the whole hospital," Eric said. "We can get into this hospital whenever we want. But I don't think I'll ever want to come back here again."

9:00 P.M.

Minutes and hours dragged on. I paced and watched the clock. What if he died? Or lost his leg? I couldn't keep these awful thoughts from my mind.

We stayed close to each other and waited into the night for the surgery to end. Eric put his head on my shoulder. Reed paced the room. Michael stared at the fish in the tank. "I'm really mad at that shark," he said.

9:30 P.M.

We heard the sounds of the elevator, and another doctor appeared. He was neatly groomed with dark hair and a seriousness that gave him an air of efficiency. His dark eyes were penetrating and intense, and his sincerity inspired trust.

"My name is Dr. Attaran. I'm the Plastic Surgeon on the surgery team. I'd like to give you an update on your son."

I rose to my feet. "Have you finished the surgery?" I blurted out.

"No-o, I'm afraid not…it's taking longer than expected. We just turned him over, and the injuries to the back of his leg are worse than I anticipated. Some of the major muscles are torn and the shark swam away with some of Jonathan's muscle in its mouth. There will be some noticeable loss."

Clinical terms blurred together… I tried to write them down… tensor fascia lata…vastus medialis…lateralalis…femoris…patella tendon. I was in over my head. Nothing was making any sense to my tired brain.

"Dr. Davis, the orthopedic surgeon, is working to repair Jonathan's knee," Dr. Attaran explained. "When he finishes, I'll suture the remaining damage to the thigh."

"What about the outcome? Is there a chance he might lose his leg?" I wondered if he was holding back details that might alarm us.

"I can't make any promises right now. We're doing our best. I talked to Jonathan when he arrived at the hospital. He was composed and articulate, even with the intense pain. You have a remarkable son. You should be very proud of him," he said as he turned to head back to surgery.

Yes, I was proud, and I simply had to trust the doctors.

"I guess that's as close as we're going to get to any reassurance," Reed said.

10:00 P.M.

A tall familiar figure appeared in the waiting room. Jonathan's friend Sean seemed exhausted and anxious. His thick black hair was tousled and blown by the wind and saltwater of the ocean. He still wore his board-shorts, t-shirt, and sandals, dusted with grains of sand from the beach that afternoon. He was a strikingly handsome young man in any setting, but he looked like he'd rather be anywhere else. He gave me a hug and sat down nervously.

"How's he doing?"

"Well, no details so far," Reed said.

"What about you, Sean? Are you okay?" I asked.

"Yeah, but I'm really worried. I saw his leg…. It was awful…"

"Sean, what happened at the beach?" Reed asked. "We're still trying to piece it together."

Sean looked uncertain and shaken. It hadn't been an easy day. He seemed bewildered.

"We have plenty of time to listen while we wait for Jonathan," Michael said.

"Okay…well…we headed out to Stinson to ride the waves and somehow a shark ended it all. I'm still trying to figure out how."

"You mean you didn't see it?"

"No, I never saw the shark. It happened so fast." His eyes looked into the distance.

"It all began when Jonathan picked me up at my house in Mill Valley. I didn't have a wetsuit and I wanted to rent one, so we stopped at the Live Water Surf Shop in Stinson on our way to the beach. The lady in the shop said she couldn't rent me a wetsuit because I wasn't eighteen. I told her I'd be eighteen in a few months and I'd pay for it, but she still said no.

So, Jonathan bought a *"No Shark"* sticker for his car – the one with a shark and a diagonal line through it – and then we left the shop without a wetsuit. I was bummed, but I decided I'd be okay in the water without it, at least for a while until I got too cold. Jon seemed surprised that I didn't mind. He reminded me I'd get cold pretty fast in that 55 degree water, but I didn't want to miss a day in the ocean after we'd driven all the way out there.

We parked near the path to the beach, grabbed our boards, climbed to the top of the dunes, and then raced across the beach with our boards. We hit the water and paddled hard to get out past the breaking surf where we could float and wait for a good wave."

Sean stopped and looked at the walls around us as if trying to remember something he had seen.

"I noticed two fishing boats anchored near the beach and saw them hauling in a big salmon. Seagulls fluttered around looking for scraps in a flurry of activity at the surface of the water, but I didn't think about what else might be out there.

Still, I guess I had an eerie feeling about the water. I'm not sure why. Maybe it was the shadows in the surf. Maybe it was just my imagination. I just wasn't comfortable out there. We caught some good waves, but I was getting cold so I yelled to Jonathan then headed back to shore to warm up. He said he just wanted to catch one more good wave...and he'd ride the next one in.

I headed for the beach and he turned back to face the ocean. When I got to the spot where we'd left our gear, I picked up my towel and looked out, trying to find him. Just then, I saw him get knocked off his board and disappear under the water. It looked like a wave had knocked him off his board, but there was no wave and I didn't know what was happening."

This time Sean squinted as if trying to make out something in the distance.

"From the shore I could see only shadows of dark water. Nothing on the surface. I knew he was a good swimmer, and I couldn't imagine why he'd suddenly disappeared. I watched and waited for him to reappear. Finally, he popped up and started paddling toward shore yelling for help. 'Help... I'm serious, I really need help,' he yelled. I could hear his voice, loud and low, over the sound of waves, but I still didn't know what was going on.

I raced across the sand and by that time he'd made it to shallow water on his own. He looked totally wiped out...He looked up at me and gasped, 'It was a shark.' His face looked really pale. He was in so much pain he could barely speak. Then I saw his leg. The water around him was turning red.

Within minutes the lifeguard was there. 'I'm Pat, and I'm here to help,' he said. He told me he'd already radioed for emergency support and the helicopter was on its way. He knew exactly what to do. He laid two boogie boards end to end and with the help of a few others we carefully lifted Jonathan up onto the dry sand, away from the waves."

Sean winced as he went on, as if thinking about it was painful for him too.

Jonathan was really struggling to stay calm and he looked awful. He wasn't saying much, just trying to focus on the pain. There was nothing I could do. His leg was torn open and his kneecap looked all shiny and white, and he looked really weak. I was pretty scared.

He tried to sit up to look at his leg. I quickly covered his eyes with my hand. I said, 'Don't look, Jon, you don't want to see it.' Then I eased him back down onto the sand. I didn't want him to see how bad it really was. He closed his eyes and tried to deal with the pain. His leg was bleeding and he looked pretty ragged lying there on the sand.

Then I heard someone yelling, 'Shark Attack.' All the swimmers rushed to shore and mothers pulled their children closer. Everyone huddled together watching. The familiar sounds of the beach suddenly changed. I could hear the ambulance and fire trucks racing toward the beach.

'Ohh...Can't you give me something for the pain?' he begged. But the lifeguards couldn't give him anything until the paramedics checked his vital signs. He had to lie on the beach and just endure the pain.

When the paramedics arrived, they rushed over to him and I stepped back. I was feeling kind of weak so I sat on a log and waited. They tried to strap him to a back board, but without any muscles to hold his leg together he cringed in pain and they released the straps. The next thing I knew, they loaded him into a helicopter. The big rotors started to turn, blowing sand in all directions. Then helicopter lifted off above the beach and disappeared over the hills."

We all sat in silence for a while, stunned by what Sean had told us. Finally I was able to speak.

"Thanks, Sean, for being there and trying to help him. I can't imagine it," I said.

'There wasn't much I could do to help. I hope he's okay."

"Imagine how you would feel if you knew
a big white shark was hunting for food
and YOU are its next meal."

- KNBC News Los Angeles

10:30 P.M.

The hospital was dark and empty. The guard patrolled the corridors. It was almost eleven when I realized how long the surgery was taking. I looked at Reed, not wanting to break the silence.

Finally I whispered, "I wonder how much longer it will be...Do you think it's worse than they told us?"

"Whatever happens, we'll help him." Reed said. I cherished Reed for being positive and strong. I was reminded how I could always count on him, and I felt better.

11:00 P.M.

Evening moved into night. Everything was quiet. Michael and Eric leaned into each other on the sofa. I could see them sinking into exhaustion. Finally, fatigue hit.

"This is taking forever. I can't keep my eyes open.... When is the surgery going to be finished?" Michael asked.

I didn't do a good job of hiding the fact that I was surprised by his impatience. "Michael," I replied, "We just have to wait. Don't forget... it's your brother's life that's on the line?"

My reminder brought him quickly back to the seriousness of the situation.

"I'll try to stay awake no matter how late it gets. I want to see him when he gets out."

"It shouldn't be much longer," Reed said, trying to be optimistic.

"Will I have to go to school tomorrow?" Eric asked.

"No, I don't think so, this is more important."

"Good, because I don't think I could concentrate."

"I think Jonathan will be okay," Michael said, staying close to Eric, and trying to hide the fact that he was worried too. Through our fatigue we waited and wondered about this wild creature that had entered our lives so unexpectedly.

11:30 P.M.

Finally, I heard the elevator doors open again. The sound echoed in the corridor. Jenan, the young nurse we'd met so many hours ago, came to speak to us, still wearing her surgical mask and cap.

"I'm staying beyond my shift because I want to help him," she explained.

"How is he doing?" I held my breath waiting for her answer.

"They're finishing up the surgery. It shouldn't be much longer. He's an amazing young man. That's why I stayed."

Her words brought tears to my eyes and I thought perhaps she was crying too. I was grateful and I hung on every word. She returned to surgery and we continued to wait.

Midnight

It was almost midnight when Dr. Davis appeared again, this time without the surgical mask.

"Jonathan is resting in the recovery room. I'll take you there now."

We followed Dr, Davis to the doorway, where he paused and turned to us. "This might be difficult for you. He's been through a lot." My heart dropped.

Reed, Michael, Eric, and I followed him down a maze of hallways and through another swinging door. I felt a cool rush of air as we walked quietly into the room. I held my breath.

My eyes wandered over the dimly lit room. Fluorescent lights cast a hollow glow. Doctors and nurses came and went, busily checking things I hadn't yet begun to comprehend.

At last I saw Jonathan, motionless in the narrow bed in the center of the room, surrounded by equipment, tubes, and IV bottles. Nearby, monitors flashed with colored messages. Red lights flashed and bobbing needles twitched on the gauges near the bed.

Everything looked unfamiliar. A silence hung over the room, interrupted only by the soft voices of nurses and doctors. They leaned over him, showing their concern even now that the surgery was over. "It's going to be touch and go for awhile until he's out of danger," Dr Davis whispered.

We tiptoed closer to the bed where Jonathan lay unmoving. He was sleeping, drained of strength and energy. I could hear his shallow breathing.

A confusing array of bandages and tubes crisscrossed his body. Despite my efforts to contain my emotion, tears welled in my eyes. I held Eric's hand and noticed tears in his eyes too.

Jonathan's leg was a web of stitches and staples, exposed to the air without bandages. Long plastic tubes came from inside the skin, draining fluid out of his leg into small plastic receptacles. His skin was stretched tight to pull together the gaping wounds and torn muscles.

"You can see the shape of the jaws on the top and bottom of his leg," Dr. Attaran pointed to the arc-shaped incisions. "The shark's teeth were like razors, so sharp they slashed straight down to the bone. His skin was ragged, so I tried to piece it together in the best way I could. Beneath the skin are more stitches, four or five layers deep."

I looked at the rows of tiny black threads, tied in knots, protruding everywhere. It looked like the work of an artist who'd created something beautiful out of something awful. Teeth marks punctuated the maze of lines in the shape of the jaws.

Large staples held his knee together and a screw inserted below his knee reattached his tendon to the bone to stabilize his kneecap. His knee was swollen to many times its normal size, red and puffy where it was pulled and stapled together. The rows of stitches that crossed his skin from his knee to his hip traced the marks of the teeth. He was a jigsaw of stitches and staples. Thin bloody lines traversed his leg, drawn together by black threads. The cuts looked fresh and new, with bits of skin pulled together, still red along the cuts. One painfully long gash ran all the way up the side of his leg to his hip. He was still asleep, probably the anesthetic, I thought. I watched and listened, afraid to say a word.

"Jonathan..." Reed said softly, hovering over his injured son, tenderly touching his hand. I waited.

Jonathan recognized the familiar sound of his dad's voice. His eyes flashed open and he looked up into our faces. His face and eyes looked puffy and swollen, especially when he smiled, yet seeing him was the most wonderful sight I could imagine, and the best thing that had happened since we arrived.

"Hi," he said as his eyes moved from one face to the next. When Jonathan looked at me, his smile lit up my life. At the same time, my heart sank to see my son injured and weak. We were teary, proud, worried, and thankful to see him.... Our lives so intertwined, nothing else mattered.

He searched the room trying to make sense of his surroundings. He studied everything, as if he were a little boy again, trying to absorb where he was and what was happening.

"...Jonathan, you've had some surgery to fix up your leg." Reed continued. "We're all here....and you're okay now." Reed was doing a good job, trying to ease him gently out of the fog of surgery and help him remember where he was.

His swollen face looked pale in the eerie white light but his deep brown eyes were commanding and strong. He was flat on his back, unable to move, and yet he looked resilient and self-assured.

"You're at the hospital now.... You've just had a long operation and the doctors are taking good care of you. Do you remember what happened?"

"Yes," he said.

He seemed composed and calm. He didn't move at all, but his eyes were shining with pride. I was overjoyed to see him radiant and awake, but I didn't want to overwhelm him, so I waited for him to respond to our presence.

He raised his arms, inviting our hugs. Reed, Michael, Eric, and I en-circled him with hugs and love, taking care not to bump his battered body. We were all there for him and we would always be there for each other. I could see the gratitude in his eyes.

A tremendous sense of relief came over me. Finally I could breathe again. After long anxious hours, Jonathan's smile answered my prayers. I'd been praying for a miracle, and now I realized Jonathan's life was our miracle. I wept silent tears of joy. Seeing him there was a sight I'd never forget.

"What time is it now?" he asked, still drowsy and exhausted.

"It's about midnight," Dad said. "You've been in surgery since you ar-rived at the hospital."

"Wow, it seems like only minutes since the helicopter landed. I guess I was asleep for a long time."

"I'm so proud of you, Jonathan, and so glad you're safe," I said. Silently, I wondered how he'd survived.

"I'm sorry I worried you, Mom," he said. "I guess it's been a long day for all of us."

Jonathan smiled and his face beamed. His spirit was amazing. He was weak and battered and stitched together, but he was thinking about our feelings and his smile gave me reason to rejoice. I thanked God we could be so fortunate.

"Let's try to make you comfortable," said Jenan, raising the head of his bed ever so slightly. Beth, Dr. Wong, Dr. Davis, and Dr. Attaran were all there, ready to help. Jonathan looked painfully uncomfortable with his injured leg extended and motionless. He was unable to move, but at least his leg was still a part of him.

"What can I do to help you feel better, Jonathan?"

"Just being here is good, Mom."

I smoothed his tangled, salty hair. I felt his feet to see if they were warm.

"Your cool hands feel good, Mom," he murmured. "I'm glad you're here with me."

"Me too."

I brushed away the grains of sand still clinging to his face and hair and even inside his ears. I was surprised at how sandy he was even after all these hours. I thought of the struggle he'd endured in the ocean, yet I couldn't imagine how violent it must have been.

Eric stepped close to Jonathan's bed. He seemed so small next to his big brother. Perhaps it was the childlike innocence I saw in his eyes as he tried to understand. Jonathan, the one who'd always helped him, played with him, snuggled with him, was flat on his back unable to move.

Eric looked at all the bandages and tubes covering Jonathan's leg. A shark attack was a lot to comprehend, especially when it happened to your brother.

"Jonathan?"

"What?"

"I guess you beat the shark. Good job," Eric said.

"Thanks." Their eyes met. Jonathan reached out for Eric's hand, to reassure his little brother. They were buddies. Eric held Jonathan's hand as firmly as he could, trying to comfort Jonathan, loving him, trying to be strong in return.

"I won't let go as long as you need me, Jonathan."

"You're a great brother, Eric."

Michael was uncharacteristically quiet. He'd hardly said a word since we'd stepped into the recovery room. He was busy looking around at everything with wide eyes, checking out all the medical devices that were hooked up to Jonathan. Michael always noticed every detail. He was fascinated by all this technology and equipment in one room.

Michael was still trying to figure out how everything worked when Jonathan looked over and spoke to him.

"Pretty cool, huh, all this stuff they've got hooked up to me?"

"Yeah, this hospital's got all the latest.... I wonder how long you'll have to stay hooked up."

"I dunno, but it's okay for now."

Michael looked at Jonathan's leg and thought about it for a minute. He looked angry.

"You know, Jonathan, I'm really mad at that shark for trying to eat you," Michael said. "I wish I could go out and hunt that shark and catch it and eat it for dinner, like the ancient Hawaiians used to do. When someone was attacked, they jumped in their boats and went after the shark."

Jonathan's smile widened. "I guess it's a good thing we don't have a boat."

"Anyway, Mom taught me revenge is not a good thing. So I forgive the shark for making a bad choice of meals," Michael said.

Reed stepped aside to talk to the doctors. I could hear him asking questions in his very thorough way. He'd ask every single question until he was satisfied Jonathan was receiving the best possible care. I could depend on Reed.

"What were the procedures you used…the outcome of the surgery… the condition of Jonathan's leg?" Reed asked. "What are his chances for recovery and what should we expect?"

Dr. Attaran explained the injuries and all the muscles to Reed, but I wasn't listening to the details that closely. It was too much information for me right now. I wanted to give my attention to Jonathan.

"We need to keep a close eye on these wounds," Dr. Attaran said. He pointed to the maze of stitches on Jonathan's leg. "Do you see this bit of flesh that looks like an island surrounded by stitches? It's connected by only the thinnest strip of skin… I'm watching, hoping the blood supply will reestablish itself and it can heal without a skin graft."

I stared at Jonathan's leg punctuated by tiny black threads poking through his skin. Now that he'd survived, what would happen next? Our life was unfolding hour by hour, day by day, and heartbeat by heartbeat.

"I've rechecked the injuries, the stitches, and the pin that reattaches the tendon to his knee," Dr. Davis said. "I've ordered heavy doses of antibiotics in case of infection. I'm optimistic because he's young and strong."

His optimism gave me hope. I hung on every shred of good news. "The signs are good and the doctors are hopeful," Reed said, giving me a hug, as if I'd done something right.

"I'm Dr. Wasserman…I'm a specialist in infectious diseases. Jonathan's entire leg is inflamed and warm. That's normal for now, but there's still the serious possibility of infection…I'll be watching him closely."

"Thank you," I said, but thank you seemed totally inadequate.

Carolyn, one of the nurses, checked the monitors and his temperature. "You're doing well," she said to Jonathan. The flashing lights on the monitors worried me. A fever could indicate an infection that would compromise his healing. I watched anxiously and prayed that Jonathan's fighting spirit would bring recovery.

Finally Reed turned to Jonathan. "You don't need to worry… you've got the best doctors," he said, giving Jonathan an extra boost of confidence.

"Thanks, Dad. I'm glad you're keeping track of everything, like you always do."

"You're here now and you're safe. Just rest and get strong," Reed said.

Jonathan looked more relaxed. For the moment, the morphine they'd given him was helping.

Our friend Ken had been standing at the side of the room, waiting quietly, not wanting to intrude, yet supportive just by his being there. Finally he started to joke with Jonathan.

"Hey, you're famous now," he said with his familiar chuckle. "You're on every TV channel in the Bay Area."

"Really?" Jonathan seemed surprised.

"The press loves your story. You're a celebrity already without even trying. That's how I heard about you and the shark…on the news. You did a good job fighting that shark." Jonathan's weary eyes sparkled as he acknowledged the compliment.

Sean came into the recovery room with his mother, Connie. She was quiet and pretty, with dark hair and soft curls. I could see the resemblance between Sean and his mother. Our boys were best friends, but I'd never met her before tonight.

"Are you and Jonathan okay?" she asked me.

"Yes, I think so," I said hopefully, but I wasn't so sure. I wondered what the next few hours would bring.

Sean looked exhausted and worried. At first he didn't say anything, and then he grinned broadly when Jonathan looked up at him.

"Hey, Jon," Sean said. "How are you doing?"

"Well, I survived!" Jonathan replied with a smile, happy to see his friend.

"Thank God you're alive. I was worried about you."

"I guess we didn't expect our day at the beach to turn out like this."

"I felt awful seeing you like that on the beach. Well, I guess you showed that shark."

Sean's presence was encouraging, but he seemed quiet and uncomfortable.

"Don't worry, there was nothing you could do," Jonathan said, anticipating what Sean wanted to say.

"At first I couldn't figure out what happened. I felt terrible when I saw you lying there on the beach...Sorry I wasn't out there in the water to help you."

I began to sense that Sean felt guilty for abandoning his friend in the water. He'd been cold without a wet suit, so he'd gone back to shore, but who would ever have anticipated something like this?

"It's okay, no one could possibly have expected it. It wasn't your fault."

"Hey, I'm just glad you're okay. I wish I could have helped you more," he said.

"Don't worry, you were great."

"Your board has a few bite marks in it." Sean smiled. "And they kept your wetsuit with the teeth marks. The shark experts want to study it."

"That's cool."

Connie put her arm around my shoulder. "Will you be alright?"

"Yes...Thanks, I really appreciate your support."

"Sean starts school tomorrow and it's getting late," she said. "So I think we'll go home. Please let me know if there's anything I can do...We moms need to stick together."

I'd be okay as long as I could be with Jonathan. We all stood close, huddled around him, forgetting how tired we were. I felt the glow of our lives intertwined with his. I held his hand. Being with Jonathan in the recovery room that first hour was as magical and precious as the hour he was born. I didn't want to leave his side.

"Jonathan, you can rest now," Reed said. "We're here with you and you're safe." No one was stepping away from that bed until we knew he was okay.

Our familiar voices blended together while Jonathan drifted in and out of sleep. We stayed close to him and to each other, thankful to be together again.

1:00 A.M.

The decision was made to move Jonathan from the recovery room to a hospital room upstairs. The nurses unhooked monitors, adjusted hanging IV bottles, and made sure everything was ready.

Carolyn, the nurse we'd met earlier, stepped to his bedside. "You've been through a lot," she said to him. "In a few minutes, we'll take you upstairs to your room so you can sleep."

"I'm so tired," Jonathan said softly. "I've never been so tired."

"Just rest now," she said.

"Hi, I'm Maryanne, said one of the nurses, taking hold of the foot of his bed. They wheeled him carefully, trying not to bump him, through the wide corridor, into the elevator, to a room upstairs. I was not letting him out of my sight. Jonathan opened his eyes only long enough to know we were with him.

"We went over and pulled him out, but it wasn't until I saw his leg that I realized what happened."
 - **Surfer at Stinson, Marin Independent Journal**

1:30 A.M.

Settled in his new room, Jonathan wasn't thinking about the shark. He was thinking only about the pain. He moaned and tried to sleep.

"I'll take Michael and Eric home," Ken offered, "and stay with them so they won't be alone."

"Thank you, Ken. You're the greatest," I said.

Only now, with Jonathan safe, was I willing to allow a break in the family solidarity. The support they'd shown for each other tonight had strengthened the confidence already so apparent in their young lives. I knew my boys would always be there for each other...and for me.

"Good night," I said, giving hugs to Michael and Eric. "I love you, and I'll see you tomorrow."

Reed and I stayed at Jonathan's bedside. We didn't ask questions about the shark.

Doctors checked Jonathan throughout the night, evaluating his condition and coordinating his treatment. I could tell they were concerned. Jonathan's condition was still critical.

The red light that worried me began to flash faster. I exchanged glances with Reed.

2:00 A.M

A few times, when the pain became unbearable, Reed had to talk him down, speaking to him firmly, almost harshly, in his stern, fatherly tone of voice. "Jonathan...relax...take a breath...you're okay..." trying to help Jonathan regain control. I wondered how anyone could handle such pain.

Jonathan finally drifted into sleep. I pressed my face into Reed's shoulder and tears flowed down my cheeks. This time, I didn't try to stop them. Every sob was so deep my entire being was consumed in this outpouring of emotion and relief. Everything I'd held inside all day, all the tension and the fear, suddenly came flowing out.

Reed didn't try to stop me while I cried. I think maybe he cried too. He wrapped his arms tighter and held me pressed against him for a long time. Neither one of us dared to say a word…we were so thankful. Then Reed spoke softly.

"We're lucky to have him, you know," he said.

"Yes…" I responded through my tears. "I'll never forget that."

"Now, let's try to be as strong as he is."

"I'm trying."

'I'll go home to be with Michael and Eric," Reed said. "One of us should be with them…. Will you be okay here?" He looked at me intently with his hands on my shoulders.

"Yes, as long as I'm with Jonathan I'll be okay."

"I'm Serious, I Really Need Help"
Shark victim says cries ignored at first.
- **San Francisco Chronicle Headlines**

2:30 A.M.

Jonathan woke during the night with flashes of pain and dreams of the shark. I could sense he was terrified.

"Mom…Dad…somebody….?" It took a minute before he realized where he was and seconds more before he remembered why. He struggled to come out of his dream. I had been sleeping in the chair next to him, but quickly woke up and hurried to flip on the light above his bed.

"It's okay…. I'm here, Jonathan…" I tried to calm him with the familiar sound of my voice. "Don't worry, you're safe now. Take a deep breath."

His features looked soft in the dim light. Strands of salty hair, still sandy from the ocean, created shadows on his face.

"I tried not to think about how scared I was…there was no one there to help me…I only thought about what I had to do to get away." I listened as his words flowed out.

"Mom," he said, "It was more than just the pain," he said. "An animal bigger than me was trying to eat me…and I was alone out there, so far from shore…"

I could find no words to reply. I took his hand in mine and tried to comfort him. I could hear the sound of desperation in his voice and his eyes showed a new awareness of the world.

"Mom…."

"Yes?"

"You're staying here with me all night, aren't you?"

"Yes, Jonathan, of course I'll stay. I will be right here in case you wake up."

"Thanks, Mom."

"The worst part is over now." I rubbed his shoulders until he drifted back to sleep.

A thin fluorescent light above the bed shed its yellow rays across his face. In the shadowy light, everything seemed unreal. I pulled my chair closer to his bed and sunk into its unforgiving vinyl cushions. Images rolled through my mind and I couldn't sleep. I'd always believed that if we were good and careful, nothing bad would happen. I'd believed my children's lives would be safe and easy, just like my own had been.

Alone in the thin light of sleeplessness I sifted through the worries and prayers every mother has for her child. Dear God, please keep him strong and keep us all safe.

I slipped my feet out of my shoes and let my head rest against the back of the chair. I reached out to feel Jonathan's hand against mine. Surely the world would be safe for him now. I was beginning to believe miracles could happen. Jonathan was alive. Already an answer to my prayers.

During the night, I heard Jonathan's voice again.

"Mom?" His eyes fluttered out of deep, restless sleep.

"Yes, I'm here."

"My bones are throbbing, and my muscles are burning."

This was not a dream, it was the reality of overwhelming pain. He was safe from the shark, but not from the pain. I placed a cool washcloth on his forehead as my mother always did to comfort me.

He brought his hand to mine, and let it slip away. I felt how weak he was from the ordeal.

"You're okay, but I know it hurts. Try to go back to sleep. Shall I call the nurse?"

"I guess I'm okay." He looked at me and remembered he was safe.

"It's good to have you back, Jonathan," I said. "I'm thankful you're alive."

In the moonlight, we could see one another clearly.

"Mom, I'm glad you're here."

———

Tower Lakes, Illinois where Jonathan learned to swim.

Jonathan and Michael warming up with Mom at the Tower Lakes Beach.

Michael and Eric with Grandma on her pier in Madison,
and Jonathan in the water riding a toy alligator

Jonathan, Michael, and Eric on Grandma's pier, Lake Mendota,
Madison, Wisconsin

Jonathan and Michael in the water, and Eric on Grandma's pier,
Madison, Wisconsin

Jonathan, with Michael, at our community pool in Lucas Valley, California

Jonathan and Sean at Stinson Beach

The "REACH" Medical Rescue Helicopter

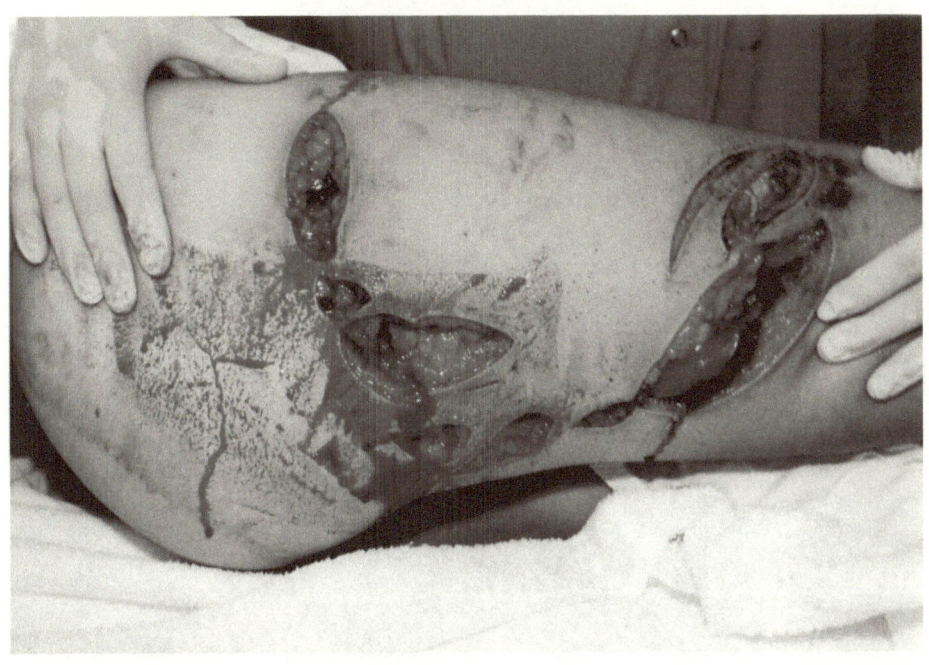

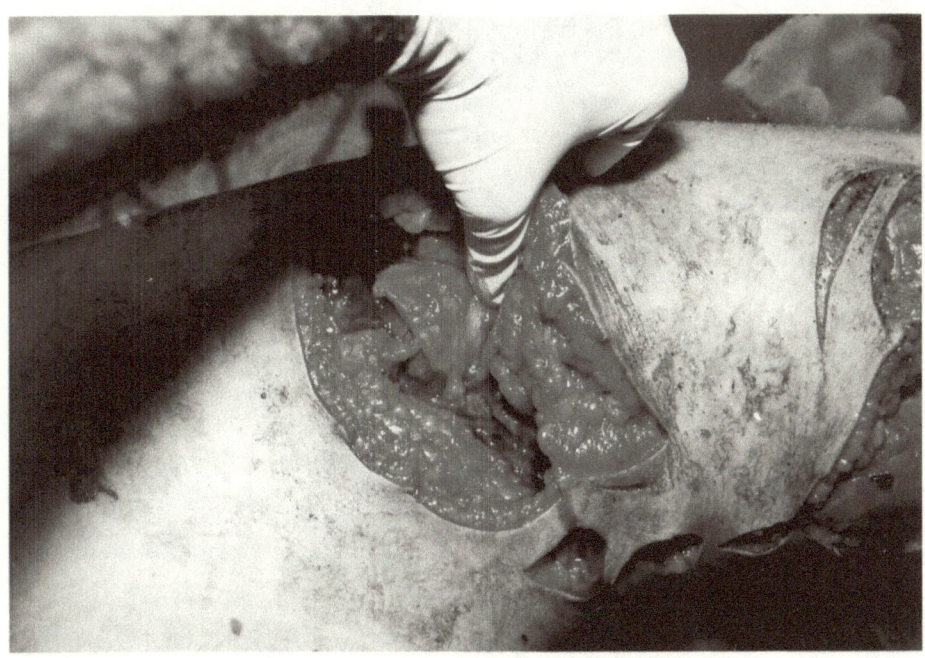

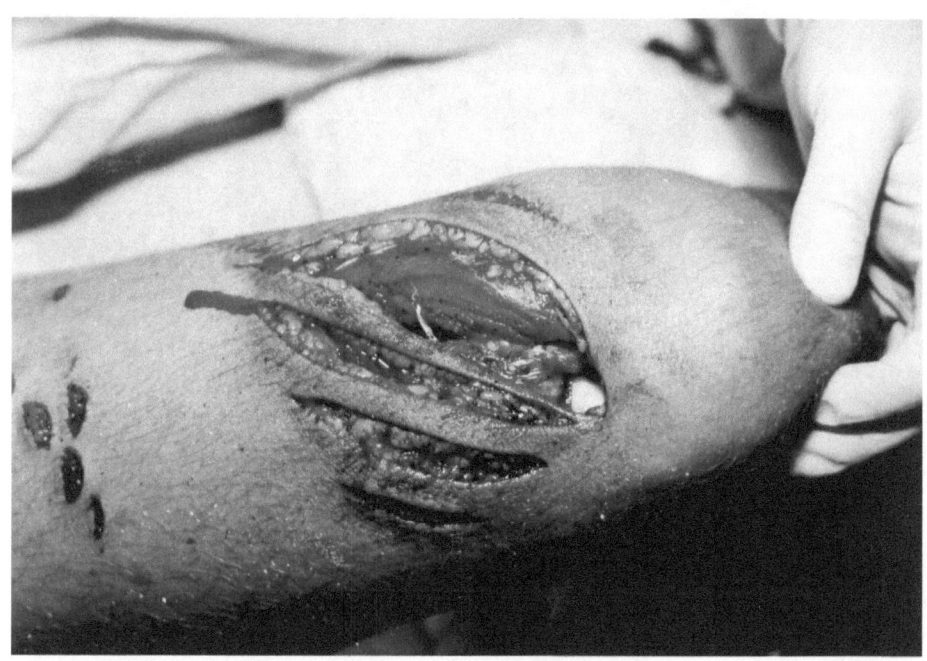

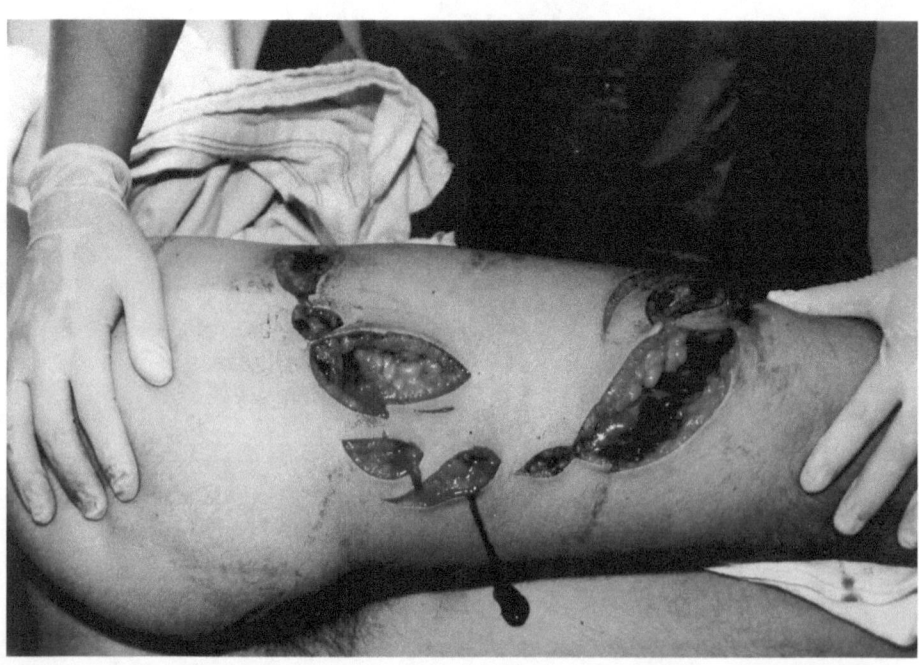

Day Two

*"Our top story... A 16 year old shark attack victim is
lucky to be alive... with experts saying
the shark was a great white...
probably out for a meal."*

\- Marc Brown, Los Angeles
ABC 7 Eyewitness News

Thursday, August 27, 1998

7:00 A.M. – John Muir Hospital, Walnut Creek

The next time I opened my eyes it was morning. I heard the sound of voices and the clatter of a cart in the hallway outside his door. I looked over at Jonathan. He slowly opened his eyes.

"Good morning, Jonnyboy," I said, reaching out to put my hand on his forehead. He smiled faintly hearing his familiar nickname. "How's my boy?"

"Everything hurts," he said as he looked down at all the stuff attached to his leg.

"Good morning to you both," said a friendly red haired nurse who bustled into the room. "My name is Coleen and I'll be your nurse for this shift.

Here's the medicine you have to take, and some ice water. Since you're only sixteen, the doctors don't want you to control you own pain medicine just yet."

"Okay, thanks," Jonathan said, taking the plastic pitcher that held the water. "I'm so thirsty I won't need a glass. I can drink this whole pitcher."

"Here you go." Coleen put Jonathan's breakfast tray on the table beside his bed, along with a stack of phone messages. I quickly sorted through them to find the ones from family and friends that needed to be answered right away and others from reporters and curiosity seekers that could wait, or not be answered at all.

7:30 A.M.

"You're here early," I said when Reed showed up in the doorway with Michael and Eric. The boys rushed to their brother's bedside.

"Had to check up on our boy," Reed said.

"We couldn't sleep anyway," Michael said. "Our phone keeps ringing."

"Yeah, and our answering machine is overloaded with messages," Eric said. "Everyone wants to know about you, so I guess you're famous, Jonathan."

The story in the morning paper quoted Michael saying, "My brother's not afraid of sharks..." They'd given Michael's words a bold slant.

"No, I said we never *worried* about sharks at Stinson."

From then on, Michael took charge of dealing with the press. Michael had read books about sharks, and remembered what he'd read. He was confident and willing to answer their questions. Michael was the point man. He decided who could talk to Jonathan, while I was busy with other things.

"I talked to the reporters downstairs in the lobby and answered some of their questions. I tried to clear up the story," Michael said. "Here are the names of the reporters you should to talk to, Jonathan, when you feel better, the ones who want real information, not just sensational news head-lines." Jonathan laughed at Michael running interference for him.

Meanwhile I was preoccupied dealing with medical concerns about his leg, healing, pain medication, and infection.

"Have you talked to the doctors today?" Reed asked.

"Not lately. They'll be back soon to check on him."

"Jonathan," Reed said, "I took your boardshorts home, the ones you were wearing under your wetsuit. They were soaked with blood and shredded by the teeth. I washed them as carefully as I could, because I thought you'd want to see them."

"Thanks, Dad, but I definitely don't want to see those shorts, not for awhile anyway."

8:00 A.M.

Jonathan slept most of the next few hours. We stayed in his room and watched over him swimming through a haze of medication, nausea, drowsiness, jitters and restless sleep. Hours passed in a fog. We could see the relentless pain overwhelm him, even in his sleep. Antibiotics and fluids dripped into his arm. Painkillers came every few hours but didn't seem to help. Tubes, stitches, and bandages covered him. Nurses monitored his condition. Whenever he opened his eyes, he looked for me.

A seemingly endless stream of doctors came through the room. Specialists in every field were called in to consult. I'd never seen so many doctors or heard so many medical terms.

Dr. Attaran stood at the side of his bed. He stopped by often to monitor Jonathan's condition and took the time to answer our questions. Already his life and ours had become intertwined as a result of the shark. I felt a sincere connection to someone we'd just met but who obviously cared about us.

"Jonathan, from the very moment you arrived at the hospital, I was impressed by your composure. You're an amazing young man to have remained so calm. You know, it's a miracle you're alive."

Jonathan smiled his shy smile. For him, it was a simple moment of pride. For me, the doctor's message underscored how fortunate we were.

"There were handfuls of sand inside your leg," the doctor said, cupping his hands. "Before we could begin the surgery, I used 6 liters of saline solution under pressure to flush the sand out of your leg. Even one grain of sand might cause an infection."

"When I ran my hand along your femur, I felt teeth marks in your bone. The shark chipped your femur. The jaws clamped all the way down. Fortunately, your leg didn't break."

"My bones are really strong because I drink a lot of milk," Jonathan said.

"All the major muscles in your leg were torn. I repaired them with stitches five layers deep. Some of the veins were as small as this tiny plastic coffee stirrer. I cut away ragged flesh and pulled your skin tight to close up the wounds. After hundreds of stitches, I stopped counting...."

The doctor's words put everything into perspective. He work was meticulous and he was tireless in his efforts. I trusted him and searched for hope.

"We were able to save your leg, but I can't give you any reassurance about how it will heal," he said. "Jonathan, your injuries were shocking, even for me, and I've seen a lot. I took some photographs of your leg before the surgery," he said. "Someday I'll let you and your family see them, but not until you're ready. Perhaps a year from now. Or maybe never."

Dr. Davis, the orthopedic surgeon, was making his rounds too. "Jonathan, your leg looked like a chainsaw or a boat propeller had ripped into it... the cuts were so destructive and deep, all the way to the bone. The shark's teeth were as sharp as a blade," he said.

"I repaired your knee with sutures and a screw to secure the tendon to the bone. I think we can save your leg if no infection occurs."

"I know it's deep because everything hurts," Jonathan said. "I'm afraid that if I move, I might pull the stitches out or tear something in my knee."

"Don't worry about that. It's a strong repair," Dr. Davis reassured him. "The suture thread I used is strong enough to pull a truck out of a ditch."

"I guess it'll be a while before I'm willing to test it," Jonathan replied with a smile.

"You'll need some hard work and rehab to strengthen those muscles. You'll have to teach the knee and leg work again. The force of impact from the jaws damaged the cartilage inside your knee, like the impact of a fall. It might never be quite the same. I don't know if you'll be able to run, but with hard work, you should be able to regain use of your leg."

"I've ordered a Continuous Passive Motion machine, a CPM machine, to be attached to your right leg," the doctor said.

"What does that do?" Jonathan asked.

"It's an electric machine that flexes and extends your leg to keep scar tissue from tightening up as it heals. We can't risk losing your range of motion," he told us. "We'll gradually increase the amount of flexing and bending each day. Our goal is to get you moving again."

Dr. Wasserman, a specialist in infectious diseases, came in after Dr. Davis. "The risk of infection remains extremely high, especially during the first forty-eight hours," he cautioned us. "Frankly there's not much research available on what bacteria might be in the mouth of a shark, or in the sand, or even in the ocean. We might not know for days how it will heal. I've ordered heavy doses of antibiotics and we'll keep a close eye on you."

Already Jonathan's room was filling with flowers and balloons. A bouquet of daisies in a yellow smiley face mug arrived from Grandma and Grandpa Marshall who sent their hugs and good wishes because they were too far away to visit. Gift certificates, cookies, and more flowers arrived from far and near. I felt the love of family and friends holding me up. In spite of all the support, nothing could truly diminish my concerns at the moment. I was positive and encouraging on the outside, but on the inside, my own emotions were chaotic.

9:00 A.M.

The CPM machine was delivered and installed on top of Jonathan's bed by a technician. His leg was strapped to this cumbersome device that flexed and extended his knee slowly with an electric motor. Jonathan cringed in pain when the motion started, but he tolerated it without complaining. Soon he accepted it as a necessary part of healing and we never turned it off, even while he slept.

Being close to Jonathan was an important part of my healing. I wanted to be there. And he needed my help with everything - the overwhelming pain, staying comfortable, drinks of water, questions from the doctors, and Tammy, with her endless flow of phone messages.

"Blood in the Water...
Teen's lesson: If a shark bites, don't forget to fight back"
                                   - **The San Francisco Examiner**

10:00 A.M.

One of the nurses turned on the TV in Jonathan's room and we all watched the morning news. A National Park Service spokesperson announced that Stinson Beach would remain closed until further notice. Authorities posted signs along the beach to warn swimmers and surfers.

The media frenzy increased. Jonathan's shark attack was headline news on every channel. Reporters were calling, eager for the story. Television newscasts showed a large billboard erected by the National Park Service at the edge of Stinson Beach warning visitors of the danger. This shark warning sign was impossible to miss:

The shark attack struck deep. The beach community was shaken, as well as communities further inland. News broadcasters expressed everyone's disbelief. Anyone who knew Stinson was shocked that this could happen at a beach that seemed so safe. Out at the beach, reporters and curious onlookers stared out to sea watching for a fin slicing the water. No one had seen any sign of the shark since the day of the attack.

We watched the ongoing TV news reports from Jonathan's room at the hospital. We heard reports and interviews by the experts.

"The shark that attacked Kathrein was probably 15 to 19 feet long with a 20 inch jaw. The shark could have easily had him for dinner," said shark expert Ralph Collier, in a live interview.

"Just look what the shark did to Jonathan's wetsuit," said David Cruz, the host for NBC Channel 4 News. "These are the teeth marks of the shark that bit the young man. This is shocking to see."

"Hey, that's my wetsuit," Jonathan exclaimed as he saw it on TV. "I haven't even seen it since the attack." Jonathan remembered someone had taken his wetsuit after they cut it off at the beach.

Ed Ueber, a shark expert from the Gulf of the Farralones Marine Sanctuary, held up the pieces of what was once Jonathan's blue wetsuit. He laid out the ragged wetsuit for the camera. "These are the teeth marks of the shark. Here we have one, two, three, four, five, six, seven, eight, nine...teeth marks," he said, pointing to each mark where a tooth had sliced through the neoprene and into Jonathan's leg. "These marks form the perfect shape of a shark's jaw."

I wondered if seeing the extent of the damage to his wetsuit and the arc-shape of the teeth marks might upset Jonathan, but he was glued to the television screen.

"The white shark attacks its prey on the surface, leaving its victim to weaken or bleed to death, then returns later to eat it," the expert explained. "If Jonathan hadn't gotten out of the water by himself, the shark might very well have circled back and eaten him piece by piece.

In this instance, the boy's buddies helped him to shore before the shark came back to get him. That's what saved his life." I couldn't listen any more. I was ready to flip the channel.

"Wait," Jonathan said from his hospital bed. "My buddies did *not* help me to shore. I swam in by myself...using only one leg. No one saved my life. I saved my own life."

Jonathan bristled at the misinformation. "The reporters are speculating about everything. My story is already distorted and this is only the first day."

"Maybe you should talk to the reporters and get it straight with them," Reed suggested. "It's all over the news, but no one has talked to you to find out what really happened."

"Oh-h-h. Right now, my leg hurts too much to think about anything." Jonathan groaned.

2:00 P.M.

"More calls for you," Tammy said that afternoon. She thrust a handful of messages into my hand.

"The press wants to get Jonathan on the evening news tonight. What do you say? Lots of reporters are waiting downstairs."

Inside, we were swept up in a whirlwind of pain, doctors, nurses, medication, and IV fluids....while outside, the curiosity of the press increased. Jonathan had fallen asleep so I decided I had to run interference for him.

"He's in too much pain and we're waiting for the doctor. His condition is still critical. Why do they keep bothering us? He can't do an interview until he feels stronger."

2:15 P.M.

"I just sent the reporters away so you could rest," Reed said to Jonathan when he awoke.

"Wait, Dad," Jonathan said. "Tell them I'll do it....I need to set the story straight. It's news today, but it won't be news tomorrow."

"Okay," said Reed. "I can see the satellite trucks below your window. The reporters are still waiting outside. I'll tell them you're ready to talk to them."

Reed followed Tammy out the door to give the okay to the reporters.

"Mom, my leg hurts so much." Jonathan cringed in agony. I wondered how he could possibly do an interview.

I pressed the nurse's call button and Colleen responded quickly. She lowered his bed to make him comfortable and gave him something for the pain.

"In an instant Jonathan's joy turned to panic...
The next seconds would decide if he lived or died."
- **KNBC Channel 4 News, Los Angeles**

3:00 P.M.

"Shall I call them in?" Reed asked.

"Yes, I think I can do it now."

As soon as Reed gave the go-ahead I heard the rush of voices from the hallway outside his door. "Folks, grab your cameras," someone said. "We have an interview."

Tammy escorted reporters and photographers into Jonathan's room. I was surprised at the number of people.

Within minutes preparations were underway for a live hookup at his bedside. Technicians set up sound gear, and microphones. Cords criss-crossed the room. Cables and hook-ups were established, ready for a live feed to begin. Photographers crowded in with video cameras and flash cameras. Microphones and lights were hastily set up. Everywhere I looked, I saw cameras, and logos, and people rushing to get this new story on the air.

Reporters moved in like the very shark they wished to portray. I heard a jumble of names as they introduced themselves... "Hi, Greg from KRON 4... Dennis from KGO...Tom from KPIX...Shannon from Hard Copy... Cheryl from ABC...Kevin from NBC...I'm Leslie from KTVU Channel 2 News... I'll be reporting on Jonathan's condition... Hi, I'm Tanya from the Chronicle....we're running a story in the afternoon edition...." There were so many names, I didn't try to keep them all in my head.

They encircled Jonathan's bed like a presidential press conference. Reed and I moved to the back of the crowded room to let Jonathan have the spotlight. Jonathan didn't need to make his entrance; he was already the center of it all.

"Jonathan, can you tell us about the day?"

Then, suddenly, the room fell silent as Jonathan began to speak. The reporters and cameramen leaned in closer. I watched as Jonathan's thoughts drifted back to the shark.

"Yes, it was foggy. It's usually foggy at Stinson Beach, and windy, but this day was unusual in many ways. There was a lot of kelp strewn on the beach. The visibility in the water was so dense something could move right past you and you wouldn't even notice. Everything was stirred up. And for some reason, there were very few people in the water. That seemed odd, but I didn't know why."

"What you were doing out there?" a reporter from Channel 4 asked.

"My friend, Sean, and I were catching waves, but after a while he got cold and headed back to the beach to warm up. I wanted to catch one more wave before heading in. I was floating and drifting out there in the swells, waiting for the waves to pick up. My legs were dangling in the deep water but I wasn't worried. Then I realized the current had carried me down the beach, and I'd drifted away from the other surfers. I was alone, so I started paddling and kicking parallel to shore, trying to get back to the center of the beach.

"Hi, I'm Leslie from Channel 2…When did you first know there was something out there in the water with you?"

"When I reached down to take a stroke, my hand hit something under the water. It felt firm and rough, like wet sandpaper. Thoughts started racing through my head. At first I thought maybe I'd hit a pile of sand underwater, but the water was too deep for that. I thought it might have been a jellyfish, but jellyfish are soft and flexible…they move when you touch them. This was firm, and solid."

"Did you think about what else it might be?"

"I thought maybe it was a seal, and I looked around hoping to see a seal pop up near me. I saw nothing but dark, empty water in every direction. From the surface, I couldn't see what was beneath me. But I knew something was out there with me."

"Were you afraid?"

"Of course I was afraid. I was terrified… alone in the ocean…50 yards from shore…I didn't know what would happen next. I knew it had to be a shark…and I had to get out of there before it came back for me. I was desperate out there in the open water, so far from shore. I turned my board and started paddling as hard as I could…trying to get back to the beach…"

"Then what happened?"

"Within seconds, a twelve foot great white shark shot up from below and plowed into my right side…It hit me at such a fast speed…and slammed into me with so much force…It threw me up out of the water… knocked me off my board…it flipped me over, pulled me down and it dragged me under water."

"Did you know what it was?"

"When it hit, I felt an explosion of pain…and tremendous force. Only a great white shark could have that much power."

The questions came quickly, and Jonathan recalled everything in vivid detail. He didn't hesitate. No longer was he a shy 16 year old. He now spoke with the confidence of someone wiser than his years.

"Could you see its eyes?"

"Hold on. I'll get to that."

"What did it feel like?"

"I felt the shark's teeth pop through my skin…and tear through the muscles of my leg…all the way down to the bone…like a kitchen knife cutting into an apple…after the initial pop of the skin, the teeth slid right through my flesh….The jaws clamped down onto the bone so tight…there was no way to escape."

Oh, my God. I couldn't bear to imagine this happening to my child.

"Did it hurt?" one of the reporters asked.

"Yes, of course…it hurt more than anything you can imagine…like getting hit by a train with a mouthful of razor blades. The pain was unbearable. The shark clamped onto my leg, and shook me until I thought my leg would come off."

"What were you thinking?"

"I was afraid it was going to tear off my leg, or drag me out to sea…I thought I was going to die. And then I got mad. I was determined to live."

At times, I saw him wince, but he didn't mention the extreme pain he was in right now, at this very moment. Instead, he concentrated on the story, and his vivid memory of the shark. He was not looking for sympathy. His face was alive with pride. He was remembering how he'd saved his own life. To me, he was the image of bravery with his windblown hair and his determined eyes. He was my hero - he'd saved himself.

"Did you try to punch its eyes," asked a reporter from KGO.

"No, I couldn't see its eyes because the shark's head and its jaws were clamped onto my leg, dragging me through the water next to it...along its side...." He paused, and everyone waited for him to continue.

"What happened next?"

"I tried to get away. But the shark held onto me with such a tight grip I couldn't pull away. Then it started thrashing from side to side, still dragging me along ...Water and sand were churning in all directions and I couldn't see. I was going out into deeper water. I felt my leg straining...."

"What did you do?

"I tried to grab the shark, but it was too big to reach around...Its body was wider than my arms." Jonathan extended his arms to demonstrate the immense size of the shark, and some of the reporters gasped. I took a deep breath and looked at Reed.

"Then, all of a sudden, I saw the shark's gills right in front of my face... about right here...I grabbed the gills, sinking my fingers into the soft flesh inside the tough outer skin. I pulled as hard as I could... trying to hold on... I was trying to stay with the shark, to keep it from ripping off my leg...."

"What did the gills look like?"

"The gills looked like big slits on the side of the shark's body, right behind its head. You've seen the tiny gills on a goldfish...well these gills were as wide as my hand. I grabbed these huge gills with both hands, like grabbing the handlebars on a bike, and pulled, trying to stay with it. I wanted to stop it from pulling off my leg."

"What was going through your head?" a reporter asked.

"I knew I had to rely on myself...I had to hold on...try to stay calm... hold my breath...and not panic...if I wanted to survive. This was my only hope to save my leg, and maybe my life. "

"Weren't you terrified?"

"Yes, I was terrified, but I had to stay focused. I couldn't think about what was happening to my leg. I knew I couldn't panic or I'd be dead."

Stunned silence swept the room. Jonathan's words hung in the air as we all tried to comprehend something so terrifying. I hardly breathed. He continued.

"Then, suddenly…unpredictably…the shark let me go. I don't know why it released me… maybe I was hurting it or cutting off its air…. Whatever the reason…it let go…all of a sudden I was out of the jaws. I bolted up into the daylight gasping for air. I found my board and started to swim as hard as I could, trying to get to shore before the shark came back for me. The shark was giving me a second chance. My only thought was to make it to shore alive."

"What about the pain?"

"The pain was unbearable. I tried not to think about it."

"Did you think someone might come to help you?"

"No one else was close enough… no one saw the shark… no one came to help me…I was out there alone …."

"Did you yell for help?"

"I shouted for help, but I didn't want to yell, 'Shark!' because no one would come to help me if they knew there was a shark in the water."

"Did anyone come to help you?"

"No, I swam all the way to shore on my own, paddling with my arms and only one good leg. When I made it to shallow water, I was still terrified. A boy swimming near shore came running and splashing over to me and tried to pull me closer to shore, out of the crashing waves. Then Sean and the life-guards helped get me out of the water. They carried me up onto the beach."

"Then what happened on the shore?"

"I was in a lot of pain, waiting for the helicopter to take me to the hospital."

"What were you thinking during the helicopter ride across the Bay?"

"I was flat on my back, staring up at the ceiling, wishing the pain would stop. I thought about my family…how much I wanted to see them…and how mom would be expecting me home."

"We're glad you survived," one reporter said.

"Me too," Jonathan smiled a broad smile.

"What advice would you give someone else who faces a shark?"

"Most of all, fight back. Keep Trying. *Never give up.* I hope something I've said today might someday help another person survive a shark attack."

"Did you ever think you'd be able to fight off a shark?"

"Well, if you think you can do it, you can." Jonathan spoke without hesitation. He'd learned he could do anything. I was amazed at his tenacity and yet, saddened with regret that my son had to struggle alone in the ocean in a terrifying attack. I wished I could erase the fear and the pain he felt.

Jonathan's face was radiant and confident. He had achieved an awareness of the world around him and of a creature the rest of us had never seen. I began to comprehend how he'd grown and changed in just one day. Most of all, he'd learned to believe in himself. As I looked around the room, I couldn't help but notice the admiration in the eyes of the reporters, focused on a determined sixteen year-old.

"When you went into the water at Stinson Beach, did you know you were entering the Red Triangle, the most heavily inhabited great white zone of the Pacific Ocean?" one reporter asked.

"I'd never even heard of the Red Triangle," Jonathan replied. "It wasn't marked on any of MY maps."

"Will you ever go into the water again?" they asked.

"Yes, I want to go back to the ocean to surf." Jonathan smiled and looked over to me.

"I guess we'll see what your mom and dad have to say about that later."

"Do you think your mom will let you go back into the ocean again?"

"We haven't really talked about that yet," he laughed.

"Will you ever feel comfortable in the ocean again?"

"I can't let this one experience stop me. I love the water and I want to surf, but probably not at Stinson," Jonathan said with an even wider smile.

"Any advice for the kids out there who might want to try surfing?"

"Yes, never surf on the last day of summer." He smiled, and the reporters smiled too.

"Okay, one last question," said Greg from KRON Channel 4. "The National Park Service issued a news release today saying there were unconfirmed shark sightings at Stinson earlier this month. Don't you think the beach should have been closed?"

I was shocked. I hadn't heard anything about earlier shark sightings. Reporters stirred the debate. I listened to the undercurrent of questions.

"Stinson Beach sits squarely in the Red Triangle, the most dangerous shark zone of the Pacific…Shouldn't something have been done to prevent the attack?" Tanya from the Chronicle asked.

"Jonathan, do you think Stinson Beach should have been closed to anyone entering the water?" Reporters prodded and probed for a storyline.

"We know sharks live in the ocean," Jonathan replied. "We can't expect the beach to be closed just because there's a shark…"

"Don't you blame the authorities for not giving stronger warnings about sharks at the beach?"

"No," Jonathan said. "It wasn't their fault. It wasn't anyone's fault. "How could anyone have expected a shark attack at the beach?"

"You're his mom…Don't you think the beach should have been closed?" The reporters looked at me. It was a question everyone was asking.

"I'm so grateful Jonathan's life was spared," I replied, "I don't want to question anything or anyone involved…everyone helped him. Most important of all, he's alive."

Another reporter persisted, "As a mother, don't you blame anyone for what happened? Don't you blame the lifeguards… the surfers… his buddies…anyone?"

I didn't have to stop and think. There was no question in my mind. "No, I don't blame anyone. Just the opposite, I am thankful for the lifeguards, friends, and people at the beach who helped him, and I'm thankful for good care from so many doctors."

I could feel the pressure to find fault. The reporters wanted headlines. But, in fact, I never blamed anyone for what happened to Jonathan. I could never blame the lifeguards who helped him. It wasn't their fault. I certainly could never blame the doctors who gave him excellent medical care to repair the massive wounds. We would never blame Sean or the other surfers, it wasn't their fault either. So who was there to blame?

"What about the shark, aren't you mad at that shark, Jonathan?"

"I was in the shark's home and I don't want anyone to resent the shark or the ocean," he said. "The shark was not to blame. The shark was living peacefully in its own world. Perhaps it thought I was the intruder in its world. Maybe it was all just a big mistake."

Finally, Cheryl from ABC 7 put away her microphone. "Well Jonathan," she said, "we don't want the interview to end, but you must be exhausted."

"Yes," he smiled. "There's much more to the story, but it looks like I'll be here for a while. Maybe we can continue another day."

"Is there anything else you'd like to say?"

"I'm just glad I'm alive...."

The reporters rushed out to get the story on the five o'clock news. I'd expected the interview to last only a few minutes, but the reporters had been mesmerized. In the end, he'd talked for over an hour. The minute they left the room, Jonathan fell asleep.

"Courage is like a kite, an opposing wind raises it higher."
- Anonymous

5:30 P.M.

"I'm really proud of you, Jonathan," I said when he awoke. My pride in my boys was something I always tried to impart to them. I thought of the melody sung by Mr. Rogers on his children's television show when the boys were young. The same words and the important message were still true, "I'm proud of you...so proud of you."

"Thanks, Mom, but the interview was the easy part. I just told my story. Fighting off the shark was the hardest thing I've ever done."

"Well, you've captured everyone's attention. You're in the news, and they're calling you a hero because of your presence of mind out there in the ocean."

"Really? Well that's cool, but I just did what I had to do," he said. "Now I hope my leg gets better. I don't care about the spotlight. All I want right now is for the pain to stop."

> *"The incredible survival story of a California teen*
> *who came face to face with the ocean's*
> *most feared predator."*
>
> - Sharon Williams,
> NBC News, Los Angeles

6:00 P.M.

Jonathan's hospital interview aired on the evening news. Reed, Michael, Eric and I watched in his hospital room. Jonathan was so tired he slept through it.

8:00 P.M.

"Visiting hours are over," Reed said. "I'm taking Michael and Eric home for tonight. What's important now Jonathan is for you to rest and get strong."

"Bye, mom. Bye, Jonathan, see you tomorrow," Michael and Eric said, and we gave each other long, tight hugs. They looked tired too. It had been a long day for everyone.

After they left, I went downstairs to the newsstand in the hospital lobby and bought a copy of each newspaper and went back upstairs to his room. His story was front page news, but he didn't care about any of that. I noticed the headlines, "Shark Attack at Stinson Beach…" and one that boldly said, "Blood in the Water…" and another said, "I'm Serious, I really need Help." I read only a few lines and piled them in the corner. I was too tired to look at them.

"Mom, you're staying aren't you?"

"Don't worry, I'm not going anywhere. I'll be right here if you need me."

His hospital room was never completely dark. There was the yellow glow from the panel above his bed and a faint light from the hallway, with nurses slipping in and out during the night. It seemed like an unreal world, pale and eerie, but Jonathan was here, safe with me, and I savored our togetherness. Just as when he was a baby, I didn't want to leave him for even a moment. The thin line between safety and danger was much too close right now. After hearing his interview, I was more thankful than ever to be near him.

Day Three

Friday, August 28, 1998

7:00 A.M.

Friday morning began with Jonathan in agony. I knew it would be another excruciating day.

"Oh Mom, my leg really hurts...every bone and every muscle in my body aches."

"Yes, honey, I know. I'll call the nurse."

This was the reality of a shark attack and there was little I could do to make things better. The medication had worn off while he was sleeping and now pain spiraled through his body. I knew it hurt terribly, I could see the tension in his face. I felt helpless.

Coleen appeared immediately. "I brought two pain pills. It might take some time before they take effect," she said. For now, nothing seemed to help.

A few minutes later, she returned with a breathing device. "Try taking a deep breath, then blow into this tube. Focus on your breathing, rather than the pain." It was a difficult challenge, but he was determined to deal with pain that came in waves like the ocean. His spirit was strong, but his physical condition was still tenuous.

> *"This young man came face to face*
> *with a great white shark and lived to tell about it."*
>   - Ross McGowan, Fox "Mornings on 2"

8:00 A.M.

Jonathan agreed to do another live interview, this time for a local news show, *Mornings on 2.* So he was wired with a microphone in his hospital bed and the crew set up the remote connection with a television camera in his room. Ross McGowan, the host of the show, interviewed him from the television studio in Oakland.

"Good morning, Jonathan...Can you tell us what happened out at Stinson?"

I hardly breathed as I heard Jonathan describe his attack again. It wasn't any easier to hear the details a second time. I was terrified... and yet he was calm.

"Before the attack, were you afraid out there in the water?" I heard Ross ask.

"No, I've always loved the water. The ocean is always beautiful..."

I'd heard him say it many times..."Mom, the ocean is always beautiful...." He'd taught me to appreciate the unexpected beauty of the ocean, in any conditions...even when the waves were wild and the fog was thick. I'd never forget his message, especially now.

"Aren't you mad at the shark?" Ross asked.

"No," Jonathan said, "How could I be mad? I was the intruder. The shark was living peacefully in its own world. I'm happy it finally let me go."

Even now, flat on his back, his love of the ocean was undiminished. He did not show anger for the shark. In some ways, he was more fascinated than ever, wanting to learn more.

"Jonathan, you're an amazing young man and we're glad you're okay. Thanks for being on our program today."

After the interview, the nurses rushed in to compliment him. He was happy to receive their kind words and he found comfort in the love and support of everyone around him. Jonathan was no longer a boy, he'd grown up overnight.

"I knew it was going to kill me or rip my leg off,
So I grabbed it by the gills to get it off me."
- Jonathan's interview

10:00 A.M.

Jonathan never expected the whirlwind of attention that enveloped him. News clips of his interviews appeared on every television channel in the Bay Area. Mail was starting to arrive from all over the world. Love letters decorated with hearts and flowers came from girls in Germany and Switzerland who'd seen his interview and wanted to be pen pals.

Our relatives and friends called from Iowa, Chicago, Wisconsin, and across the country. "We saw Jonathan on TV....Oh, my gosh, is he okay... we read about him fighting off the shark...It's so unbelievable...Give him a hug for us." A box of chocolates shaped like long stemmed roses arrived with a card that said, "You are one lucky mom!" These words described my feelings exactly. Another message for Jonathan said, "Congratulations to a True Survivor....We're glad you're still around to tell the tale." The cast and crew of *Phantom of the Opera* sent Jonathan an autographed poster and an invitation to attend the show.

In the midst of what might have seemed like misfortune, these sentiments reminded us how fortunate we were. As a family, we could survive this fear, worry, and turmoil in our lives. Jonathan's awareness had expanded into another realm...the world of the ocean and its creatures.

Our world had expanded too. While we were struggling to make sense of everything, the people around us helped guide us through each day.

3:00 P.M.

That afternoon our friends, Marcy and Rebecca, two moms and neighbors from Lucas Valley, came to visit us at the hospital. They brought a special journal entitled, "Dream…a Notebook of Visions." The cover was decorated with stars and whimsical images alluding to dreams of a brighter future. Inside were pages waiting to be filled with the story we were living.

"Jonathan, you're a miracle-boy," Marcy said. "You and your mom should keep a journal, and write down all your memories."

"I think writing would be a good idea," Jonathan said after they'd left. "Will you help with that, Mom?"

"Yes, of course I will. We have so much to be thankful for, and so much to remember."

"I don't want to forget anything. And I'd like to know what you were thinking while I was in surgery," Jonathan said.

"Writing will be good for us," I replied, thinking of my gratitude in so many ways.

So far, I'd been writing notes on scraps of paper – now we had a journal for our memories. That day, we began to write about the events and our thoughts as they unfolded, still trying to come to grips with a story that was unbelievable, even for us.

Our first journal entry seemed simply meant to encourage ourselves…. quoting words of the doctor, "He's lucky to be alive," and headlines from the newspaper, "Teen face-to-face with a great white shark, and lives to tell about it." The words made me feel proud. I decided we'd record comments from visitors and doctors and ask our friends to write their comments too. I wanted to appreciate and remember each milestone in Jonathan's recovery and foster our dreams for better days ahead.

5:00 P.M.

Dr. Attaran appeared in Jonathan's room late that afternoon with a serious look on his face. "Kaiser wants Jonathan transferred to their hospital in Terra Linda," he announced, walking to the side of Jonathan's bed.

"Oh no. We can't move him," I replied in disbelief. "You and the other doctors here at John Muir are the ones who saved his life. You know the depth of his wounds. I don't trust anyone else. You're his doctor. Can't you tell them he's not ready to be moved?" I was nearly in tears.

"It's all about business," Dr. Attaran explained. "I'd like to keep him here, but Kaiser Health Care is your insurance carrier, and he's a high profile patient. They want him at their hospital."

"Is it medically advisable for him to be transferred so soon?" Reed asked.

"I'll examine him later today. Unless there's a medical reason for me to keep him at this hospital, I'll have to let him go."

8:00 P.M.

Dr. Attaran released Jonathan that evening and preparations were made to transport him by ambulance to Kaiser Hospital in Terra Linda. The hospital would be closer to our home, but that was not my concern. My concern was for the care he'd receive.

Jonathan was carefully loaded onto a gurney and taken to an ambulance at the ER door for our trip across the Bay. After they said goodbye, Reed, Michael and Eric headed home. It was already getting late, and this promised to be another late night.

The ambulance crept along slowly, mile by mile, taking care to avoid jolting him. I followed the ambulance in my car, crossing the Richmond-San Rafael Bridge, into the darkness and uncertainty of another long night.

When we arrived at Kaiser Hospital, I rushed to the ambulance door.

"Are you okay? How was the ride?" I asked.

"Painful," he said. "My leg hurt on every bump and every turn."

"Well, we're here now and the doctors are expecting us."

"Jonathan, I'm glad to see you. We're going to take good care of you." Nancy, one of the nurses, was a mom we knew from Little League. She greeted us and settled Jonathan into a room. Dr. Totten, the orthopedic specialist, had stayed late into the night to examine him.

"I've studied your records and everything looks good," the doctor said. His knowledge and familiarity with Jonathan's injuries gave me the confidence I'd needed. "Don't worry," he said looking at me, as if reading my mind, "We'll take good care of him here."

The comfort of caring people along with his still-fragile condition brought competing emotions - a feeling of confidence tempered by the dull, aching sadness that this had happened at all. From the window in Jonathan's room after everyone had left, I could see the moonlight reflecting on the familiar golden hills of Marin. It did feel good to be back.

11:30 P.M.

It was our third night together in a hospital room and thoughts of losing him were never far from my mind. This close call had given each of us a greater sense of our mortality. I taped a picture of Mother Theresa to his bed because she'd helped so many people during her lifetime. I was drifting, searching for hope and healing.

Helping Jonathan struggle with pain occupied every hour of the day and night. I rubbed his forehead and held the glass of water while he drank from the straw. He was always thirsty those first few days. Probably because he'd lost a lot of blood, I thought. Even the strongest medication didn't relieve the pain. He tried to sleep, but awoke frequently, overwhelmed and frightened by dreams he didn't fully remember. I had only to look at his leg to know that this was not a dream.

Day Four

"Jonathan, I've prayed for you since
I heard about you on TV,
never knowing you'd be my neighbor in the hospital.
I know beyond a shadow of a doubt,
God has mighty plans for your life."
- Claudia, Kaiser patient, Room 509

Saturday, August 29, 1998

9:00 A.M.

The pain wasn't letting up. Sandy, our morning nurse, stood beside his bed checking the tubes, taking his temperature, recording notes, all the routine things I'd begun to expect.

"The doctor wants you to sit up today," she announced.

"Okay," Jonathan replied without questioning. I wondered how he could sit up at all, when he couldn't even move.

"I'll be right back to help you," she said as she hurried off.

A few minutes later she returned with Amy, another nurse. "Turn carefully," they said, while together they lifted his shoulders. His leg was held straight by a cumbersome black immobilizer.

"There you go," Amy said. "A whole new perspective on the world.
How does that feel?"

"Good," Jonathan replied, wincing in pain, but not complaining.

"Next thing you know, we'll have you walking." To me this seemed an
amazing prospect.

Writing our journal entries became a true collaboration. I did much of
the writing while Jonathan was flat on his back, but he was the one who'd
lived it. We noted milestones in his recovery, memories, comments from
friends, miracles to be celebrated, and facts we'd learned about sharks, the
creatures we were beginning to find so amazing. I was overjoyed whenever
we saw signs of progress and he'd say, "Mom, don't forget to write this
down."

In all my years of scuba diving,
I've seen hundreds of sharks
But I know chances of being attacked
are one in a million.
Jonathan, you are truly "one in a million."
                                    - **Grandma Marshall**

11:00 A.M.

"Hey, Jonathan," said a friendly voice. "I came to check up on you...
My name's Pat Norton, I'm the lifeguard from Stinson Beach." He stood at
Jonathan's bedside with an endearing smile and sun-streaked hair, looking
impressive in his official dark green National Park Ranger uniform. Pat
was the lifeguard who'd so skillfully coordinated Jonathan's rescue on the
beach.

"Of course, I remember you from that day," Jonathan said.

"So, how're you doing?"

"Well, much better than the last time you saw me." A laugh rolled off
Jonathan's words.

"I brought your wetsuit," Pat said. "It's been on display at the Gulf of the Farallones Visitor Center at Crissy Field in San Francisco. It has a few bite marks in it...as you would expect," he smiled. "I thought you'd want to have it back."

Pat sat on the edge of the bed and handed Jonathan his wetsuit, now neatly folded and wrapped in plastic. It was mounted on a blue display board next to a picture of a great white shark. Arrows pointed to each tooth mark in the wetsuit where the shark's teeth had penetrated and torn the neoprene, where the jaws had held him. Jonathan looked at it and studied the marks.

"The shark did a good job of tearing your wetsuit apart...," Pat said. "Now it will be a reminder for you, like a badge of courage."

Jonathan looked at it without a word. I imagined what he must be thinking.

"Lots of curious visitors came to see it while it was on display," Pat said.

"Really?" Jonathan said.

"Great white sharks are rarely ever seen, you know. Most people, even the scientists, have never seen one," Pat said. "The surfers were fascinated because you're one of the few survivors."

"I'm surprised anyone cares about a wetsuit."

"It's been studied by the top shark experts. The size and shape of the teeth confirm that it was a great white shark...not that we had any doubt. At Stinson you were in the middle of great white territory."

"Yes, I know that now, but I didn't know then."

Pat sat on the edge of the bed facing Jonathan. He spoke with experience of the ocean.

"Jonathan, you're a brave kid. You faced up to something as big as a truck and didn't lose your head. You stayed calm and fought back, that's what saved your life."

Jonathan blushed. I could see the mutual respect they had for each other. They were drawn together by their love for the ocean and the surf. And its unexpected consequences.

"Thanks for getting the helicopter to the beach so quickly, Pat. Your help made a big difference."

"You did the hard part, you saved yourself."

"Pat, can you tell me anything more about the conditions of that day?" Jonathan asked. "I'm trying to understand how everything happened."

"Yes, I remember it well. It started out as a quiet day at the beach. Waves with 3 foot faces were breaking into smooth arcs close to shore. There were very few surfers in the water. It was about an hour before high tide.

From the lifeguard tower, I could see lots of activity at the surface of the ocean. The upwelling current was in full effect. Pelicans skimmed along the water diving for fish. A seal chased a fish or was being chased and quickly disappeared. Seagulls hovered trying to pick up the extras. The ocean looked unsettled and dense. Long ropes of kelp had washed up onto the beach that night."

"Really," Jonathan said. "I didn't know the currents changed in the late summer."

"Yes," Pat continued, "In August and September there's an abundance of life close to shore. A deep upwelling current brings krill and small fish closer to shore… drawing the salmon in…the seals follow the salmon…and the sharks follow the seals. We call it shark season. The ocean is teeming with life."

"So that explains the fishing boats close to shore?" Jonathan asked.

"Yes. And you happened to be in the middle of the food chain."

Jonathan and I listened as Pat continued. "There's never been a shark attack recorded at Stinson, ever. And in all my years as a lifeguard at Stinson Beach, I've rarely ever seen sharks close to the beach. Sometimes I hear rumors of sharks, but we can't close the beach for every unofficial sighting. In twenty years at Stinson Beach, I've never seen a shark attack.

I was in the lifeguard tower when I heard you calling from out in the water, shouting for help. Your voice had a desperate quality that I'd never heard before. It sounded like a low moan that resonated across the water… a sound that could not be mistaken. I knew immediately that someone was in serious trouble. I knew it was real."

Pat remembered everything clearly. "From my vantage point in the tower, when I looked out across the surface of the water, I noticed that every head was turned in your direction, Jonathan. I could spot instantly who was calling for help. I saw you paddling frantically toward shore, about 50 yards out, in about 8 feet of water, calling and struggling to get back to the beach. I knew it had to be a shark attack. Everything was happening so fast, fortunately my years of emergency training kicked in and I knew exactly what to do.

Before I left the tower, I radioed the emergency call, requesting a full emergency response. The call went out to the Stinson Beach Fire Station, the Marin County Fire Department paramedics, the REACH life flight helicopter — and of course it was immediately picked up by the press.

Within minutes, the helicopter pilot radioed that he was in the air on his way, the Stinson Beach paramedics responded, and two fire trucks arrived at the beach. I raced across the sand to get to you. Before you were even out of the water, the rescue was underway.

By then you were in shallow water leaning on your elbows, completely exhausted. You couldn't move... your leg was bleeding profusely... and you were weak from losing so much blood. I was thankful you were alive.

We needed to get you onto dry land. I instructed Steve Hills, the other lifeguard on duty, and Sean your friend, and about five others to help me. We laid two boogie boards end to end and lifted you onto the makeshift stretcher. Your leg looked pretty torn up but I couldn't tell how bad it was. You moaned in pain, but you stayed calm and you didn't panic."

Pat became quite animated as he continued to tell us the story. "Jonathan, you created quite a stir at the beach. Steve hopped into the lifeguard truck and drove up and down the beach warning the other swimmers with a loudspeaker, 'Clear the water... Everyone out of the water!' At this point, our job was twofold - we needed to take care of you and prevent anyone else from getting hurt by the shark.

Then someone on the beach yelled, 'Shark attack!' Reality hit. Panic spread across the beach. Sirens erupted. Swimmers and surfers rushed to safety. People stood on the sand, staring out across the empty water looking for the shark.

You were in the midst of all this commotion, Jonathan. You kept your eyes open, looking straight up, waiting for help. Your buddy, Sean, tried to reassure you. 'Jon, you're going to be okay,' he kept saying. Surfers on the beach seemed nervous and shaken.

'How bad does it look?' you asked, lying motionless on the sand. 'Do you think I'll lose my leg?' I remember your asking, but at that point, we didn't know.

Another Stinson Beach lifeguard, Scott Palmer, was off duty and he happened to be on the beach that day. He saw what was happening and ran over to lend a hand. 'Pat...what can I do to help?' he asked breathlessly.

'We need to stop this bleeding...Grab some bandages,' I said.

Scott handed me the bandages. I took one look and said, 'Get bigger ones!' At least we can smile about this now.

Then a man dressed in shorts and sandals came over and knelt beside you in the sand. He said he was a doctor and maybe he could help. He was very kind and gentle, but there was little anyone could do. A circle of people gathered around you. The shark had brought strangers together on the beach. Then a fire truck arrived and the paramedics rushed over.

'Everyone please step back,' they said. They had an oxygen tank ready but first they asked you lots of questions like, 'What's you name...phone number... age?' You answered their questions, but it was tough for you, with all the pain. Then, finally, you said, 'I don't want to talk anymore. My friend Sean is right over there, you can ask him.'

'We need to make sure you're fully alert,' they replied.

'Can't you give me something for the pain?' you asked.

'We need to check your vital signs first,' they explained, rushing about. 'Just hang on a little longer.'

You closed your eyes, concentrating, trying to deal with the pain. One of the paramedics opened a first aid box, grabbed a scissors, and started to cut off your wetsuit.

'Wait,' you said, 'Can't you try to save my wetsuit? I might want to wear it again.' Kind of funny, at a time like that, you were worried about saving your wetsuit.

'Sorry, we have to cut it off,' the paramedic said. 'We've got to check these wounds.'

The paramedics were trying to determine if the shark had hit the main artery in your leg. Once your suit was off, the damage to your leg and hip looked worse than I expected. Your leg was torn open from your knee to your hip. Some muscles were gone and I could see your kneecap, a glistening white bone, and the bone in your thigh exposed. But you stayed calm and alert there on the beach, with nothing to numb the pain.

Exactly twenty-three minutes later the helicopter landed at the beach. We quickly loaded you inside. When that door slammed, the helicopter lifted off over the beach and turned inland, heading across the hills toward the East Bay. How was the ride across the bay, Jonathan?"

"I think that's when I finally began to feel safe," Jonathan said, his eyes looking into the distance as he remembered. "What I remember most inside the helicopter, was lying flat on my back, staring up at the geometric pattern in the grey ceiling above me, wishing the ride would end and the pain would stop. A nurse sat at my head surrounded by lots of medical equipment inside the tiny cabin. She told me we'd be there soon but to me it seemed like forever.

'School starts tomorrow,' I said to the nurse, 'Do you think I'll be able to go?'

'I guess we'll see...' she replied softly.

Then I heard the pilot's voice over the noise of the engine. He said, 'I've seen a lot of accidents, but never a shark attack. That shark could have torn off your leg. You're a lucky kid.'

I didn't feel lucky but I knew he was right. I'd wait to hear what the doctors said about my leg. I was afraid of what their decision might be.

The pilot said, 'We're heading across San Francisco Bay right now. We'll land in exactly twenty-two minutes at the Trauma Center at John Muir Hospital in Walnut Creek.'

'Wait...' I said, 'Why are we going to John Muir? I'm a member of Kaiser.' I was worried our insurance wouldn't cover it and I didn't want to cause extra trouble and expense for my parents.

'Don't worry,' he said. 'John Muir is the designated Trauma Center. Just try to relax.'

"I'm going to give you a shot of morphine now,' the nurse said, leaning over me looking anxious. Even morphine didn't dull the throbbing pain, but I closed my eyes. The rhythmic hum of the helicopter blades reminded me of the sound of the surf...."

"You know, Jonathan, you are a lucky kid in one big way...." Pat said. "There are no beaches anywhere north of Stinson with lifeguards." I remained silent, wondering if Jonathan had survived through destiny or miracles. As I listened, I realized how fortunate we were that Pat was there to call the helicopter so quickly, and to coordinate Jonathan's rescue.

"By the way, I brought you this souvenir." Pat handed Jonathan a faded grey t-shirt with the words, "US Park Service Lifeguard" in big red letters across the back. "It's the shirt I was wearing that day out at Stinson."

"Thanks ...for everything," Jonathan smiled.

Pat's life had intersected with ours because of the shark. We knew we'd see him again – we shared a love of the ocean, and the ocean had brought us together.

"Well, you've been through a lot, and I'm heading out to Stinson now," Pat said as he stood to leave. "People are still watching for your friend out there in the water."

1:00 P.M.

That afternoon, the San Francisco *Chronicle* ran an article with a picture of two dolls, Ken and Barbie...with Ken's leg in the mouth of a shark. The caption read, "Sharon, at the Surfers Grill in Stinson Beach is worried about the long-term effects of the shark attack." Business at Stinson was slow with fewer people at the beach.

The Surfers Grill was a favorite lunch spot overlooking Stinson Beach where, on a hot day, the line of people waiting for burgers and shakes might stretch around the corner. But now the town was quiet, the restaurant was empty, and the beach was closed.

The article said the shark attack had shaken the local surfing community. Late summer swells brought the promise of good waves, but surfing didn't seem as popular, especially at Stinson. Surfers kept a watchful eye along the coast. Curious visitors ventured to the edge of the water with cameras but no one swam or surfed at Stinson.

2:00 P.M.

The phone kept ringing. There was never a dull moment in Jonathan's hospital room, and never a break in the activity. I was glad to field the calls and visit with friends who stopped by. Often Jonathan slept through everything.

Jonathan received a book, *Cousteau's Great White Shark*, filled with color photographs of sharks, from Sharon, his childhood babysitter in Illinois. "We're thankful you'll heal and continue to bring joy and love to everyone whose life you touch," Sharon wrote in the cover of the book.

Jonathan tried to read a few pages from the book that afternoon. He wanted to understand more about sharks and the ocean. "Mom, I'm not surprised to learn that a great white shark can swim beneath a swimmer without being noticed... that's exactly what happened to me when the shark first bumped my hand." He found the shark book fascinating, but he fell soon asleep and I put the book aside for another day.

3:00 P.M.

"Hi, my name is Dan, I'm a producer for NBC," he said when I answered the phone. "We'd like to interview Jonathan for the Dateline NBC Survivor Series on national television."

"I don't think so. Jonathan doesn't want to do any sensational programs," I said firmly.

"Don't worry; we'll focus on his quick thinking and how he survived, not the sensational aspects of the shark attack."

"Do you want to do this, Jonathan?" I asked.

"Sure. But can he wait 'til the pain's not so bad?"

"Okay," I said. "We'll agree to the interview but you'll have to work around doctor visits and bouts of pain."

"Okay. I'll clear everything with the hospital and I'll have my crew there tomorrow morning. I'd like to interview each of you, to tell the story of your family and your support for one another."

"Okay," I agreed. It looked like busy days of interviews ahead. There was never any offer of compensation, and Jonathan didn't expect it. He was simply willing to tell his story.

"We'll shoot some footage of Jonathan in the hospital, and then a follow-up on the beach in a couple of months. It's going to be a great story. Jonathan embodies all the qualities we're looking for in a survivor. He'll headline our fall NBC Survivor Series."

His words confirmed what I already knew. Jonathan was truly a survivor. He was not about to give up — then or now.

5:00 P.M.

Jonathan continued to be bombarded with images of sharks everywhere he looked. Somehow he shrugged it off. Could any one of us look at the photo of our attacker each day and not let it bother us, I wondered?

Friends sent greeting cards with sharks, shark jokes and articles about sharks. Crayon drawings of sharks and surfers came from school children, and we taped them to the wall in his room. He received shark beanie babies and shark key chains. Visitors brought shark stuffed animals, shark bathtub toys, coral shark decorations, miniature sharks, a pewter shark pendant, shark swim goggles, shark books, shark bookmarks, and even a shark bath tub drain stopper. Necklaces made of shark's teeth, mostly not from great white sharks, were a popular gift. One porcelain shark figure was a music box that played, "I did it my way."

Rich, one of our friends, laminated the quote, "I'm serious, I really need help," and the photo of Jonathan from the *Chronicle,* onto a card the size of a credit card. "Carry this card in your wallet as proof, because in a few years, no one's going to believe your incredible story," he said. We appreciated the humorous gifts that lightened our traumatic experience.

Surfers in Hawaii sent a book called, *JAWS Maui*, with full-color surfing photos signed by famous big wave surfers who'd surfed the wave known as "Jaws." A scientist at Scripps Oceanographic Institute in San Diego sent his research paper documenting great white shark attacks along the California coast and around the world. John McCosker, author and world renowned shark expert, sent a signed copy of his book, *Great White Shark*, along with his personal invitation to tour his private laboratory at the Academy of Sciences in San Francisco.

Colorful balloons and flowers filled his room. We found comfort reading through the mountains of mail. The gifts and cards from well-wishers became treasured mementos reminding us of our good fortune - Jonathan had survived the day of the shark.

We continued to record Jonathan's progress in our journal whenever I could find a moment to write. Writing together gave us a sense of connection with each other and a chance to reflect on our experience. Each day became a new chapter in our emerging awareness of our relationships with people and the ocean.

11:00 P.M.

That evening, when the hospital was quiet and all the visitors had gone, I took a deep breath and looked at Jonathan, his long legs filling the hospital bed. I treasured every moment while we reminisced about memories and happy times.

"Mom, do you remember the time it snowed so much the schools were closed and we built an igloo in our yard in Illinois? Inside, it was so quiet and safe."

"Yes," I said, sharing his memories.

"I miss those winter nights when we ice-skated on the pond under the big lights and you could see your breath," he said.

These joyful memories took us to a world that existed before the shark. Memories helped us forget his terror in the ocean, and my terror of nearly losing someone so dear to me. I knew we would never again step into the ocean or share family days at the beach without remembering.

During long days and nights at his bedside, I grew to know Jonathan as a person, not just as a child. I relished my time alone with him. Staying close to him was important, almost like my own therapy too. Simple things like bringing water and comforting him helped me feel better.

I learned how awful it is to know the suffering of your child. To be powerless to prevent these things from happening. There were many questions I couldn't bear to ask about all he had endured. And yet I marveled at the grace and perception of this young man who was my son. I didn't know why he was spared or where our lives were headed, but as a family, we were forever changed. As I thought about his escape, I became more aware of God's presence in our lives.

In his own way, Jonathan taught us to become our best selves. Each day he reminded us to find joy and he taught us to live our best lives. When he faced the shark and fought back, he confronted a challenge he didn't know he could handle, showing us that we too could accomplish things we didn't know we could do.

Midnight

Late that night, I sat on the edge of his bed, as I often did at home, to talk about our day. This time, I simply listened.

"Mom, I don't know if I can ever go back to the ocean…The beach will never be the same again."

"…No, I guess it won't," I said, thinking of how we'd always felt safe at Stinson Beach. We'd never had any reason to feel otherwise, until now.

"Mom, I was just thinking about the shark…I remember every detail so clearly …"

He paused for a moment, and then everything came in a rush, almost like a flashback.

"The shark hit me so hard… it threw me up out of the water, then pulled me down with its teeth ripping into me. It was a battle for my life and I knew it. I had to fight back and keep trying. It was the worst fear I've ever known. Even after the shark let me go and disappeared, I knew I wasn't safe. Sharks can smell even a drop of blood. I knew it would circle back for me. I had to get away… fast. The next hit would be even worse… I knew I could die. I was completely alone out there in dark empty water. The other surfers had caught a wave or drifted away. They didn't know I needed help. I had to get back to the beach on my own.

I felt tremendous pain…and I couldn't move my right leg. Then I found my tangled leash, somehow it was still attached to me, and I grabbed hold of my board. It wobbled from side to side but I held on… trying to kick with only one leg and paddle with my arms…using all my strength and adrenaline…. through the choppy water… trying to get to shore. Closer to safety. But I couldn't get going fast enough. I was terrified each time I reached down into the dark water to take a stroke.

I shouted for help, but no one heard me. I prayed for a wave to carry me in…I had to get back to shore. Nothing else mattered. The water was flat… I couldn't get going…then suddenly a wave rolled toward me. Oh no, this is it… I thought the wave might capsize me. Hold on, I told myself. I clenched my board. The wave pushed me forward and I was moving toward shore. Swim…Keep swimming. Don't panic… Get to shore. I kept swimming as hard as I could and never looked back.

Finally, I reached the shallow water, gasping for air, trying to endure the horrible pain, thankful to be alive. Sean came running and splashing toward me through the water. He looked at me in disbelief and grabbed me by my arms, trying to steady me in the waves crashing near the shore.

Then a woman rushed into the water too, and within seconds Pat, the lifeguard, was at my side. Sean, the woman, and the lifeguard surrounded me, trying to help. Already I could hear sirens in the distance. I wished the pain would stop, even for a moment.

The next thing I knew, they lifted me up onto dry sand. People rushed over. I was lying on the beach, looking up into the faces of all these people hovering over me. They looked tense and worried. I was so weak I couldn't move and I didn't know what shape my leg was in, but I was alive. I closed my eyes, trying to block out the sirens and the pain."

After a pause, he continued, "Mom...."

"....Yes, Jonathan?"

"You've seen pictures and videos of sharks attacking seals...and you know how awful it looks?"

"Yes...."

"Well, this was even worse... more violent than you can imagine. The shark was shaking and thrashing me from side to side...with its teeth cutting into me. The greatest predator of all was trying to tear me apart."

I was breathless as I listened. His words conveyed a depth of courage I could not imagine. I simply didn't know how to respond to an experience so profound. I could not envision the intensity of the battle or his struggle to survive.

I held his hand. "Jonathan, how did you ever hang on?"

"I wasn't going to let it take me. I wasn't ready to die. The shark was so powerful.... it could snap my leg like a twig. I knew if that shark wanted to eat me, it would. But, somehow, it let me go." His voice drifted off for a moment.

"I always thought I'd have children and grow old," Jonathan said. "I never stopped to think it could all be taken from me....Now I realize how fragile life is and how important my relationships are to me. Mom, I just wasn't ready to give it all up."

Just then Nancy, our nighttime nurse, stepped in to check on him. "Are you still awake? I think you should get some rest. You've been through a lot." She fixed his pillow. He closed his eyes, already drifting off to sleep. I knew he'd paid a heavy price for the insight he'd gained.

As I reflected on his childhood, I realized that somehow he'd been in training for the shark attack all his life. He'd always been passionate about things he loved. He'd joined our Lucas Valley swim team, he'd practiced hard and learned to be a strong swimmer, he'd become a lifeguard at the Lucas Valley pool...And now he'd saved himself.

Days Five through Eight

"Blood in the water...
Teen's lesson: If a shark bites,
don't forget to fight back."
                                    - San Francisco Examiner

August 30 to September 2, 1998

For the rest of Jonathan's stay at Kaiser Terra Linda Hospital, each day began early with doctor visits. The phone rang nonstop with calls from reporters and shark experts. "How many stitches?" Every reporter wanted to know.

"We're way beyond that," Jonathan replied. "The doctors gave up counting."

While Jonathan slept, I read the newspapers that were piling up in the corner of his room. The "Red Triangle" had become headline news in every paper with maps showing its location. We'd never heard of the Red Triangle until now, and the thought of a shark attack at our favorite beach had seemed impossible. Now I was surprised to learn that the Red Triangle is a 100-mile stretch of the Pacific coast from Monterey Bay to Point Reyes, and out to the Farralon Islands twenty-six miles offshore from San Francisco. Scientists say this area is frequented by more white sharks

than any other part of the Pacific, with the most recorded shark attacks in
the world. And, I learned, the Red Triangle encompasses Stinson Beach.

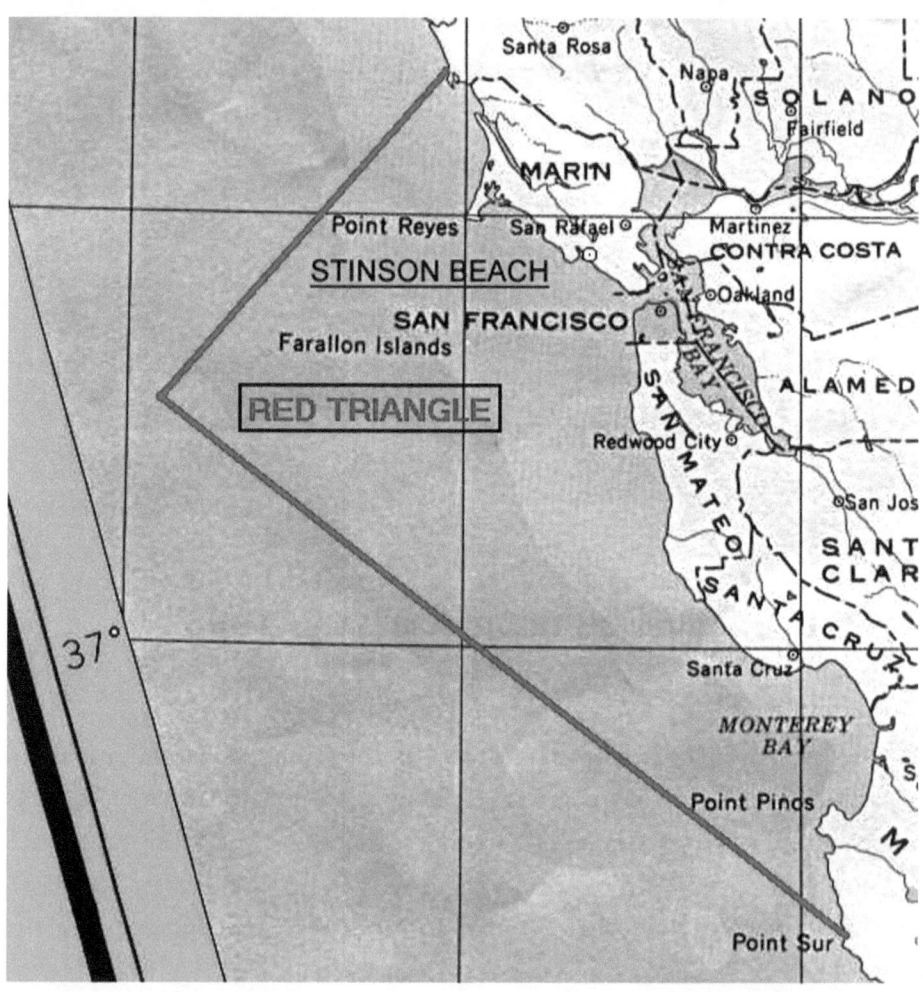

I'd seen the Farralon Islands, the tip of the Red Triangle, from the
Golden Gate Bridge. But I didn't know these rocky peaks were the home
of seals and sea lions, and the breeding ground for great white sharks. Even
though the sharks are rarely seen, the Red Triangle gets its reputation from
the number of great whites and the color of the water after an attack. But
sharks are not entirely to blame for this statistic. The number of attacks is
also the result of the great number of people in the water near San Francisco.

The Red Triangle encompasses many popular beaches where people swim, dive, and surf along the coast. An easy swim for a great white shark.

Scientists from San Francisco, Monterey, San Diego, and Florida called to talk to Jonathan about his experience. He was one of few shark attack survivors in the world. "What did the shark look like? How big was it? What time of day did it happen? What were the conditions of the water? How far from shore? How did the shark attack?" Researchers wanted to document everything and Jonathan responded with details and observations. Researchers sent us scientific studies and journal articles documenting other shark attacks. Some of these stories were dreadful and awful, reminding me how fortunate we were.

We asked questions of the experts too. We'd become fascinated by this mysterious and amazing creature that had so suddenly entered our lives. We learned that the white shark is not entirely white, but dark grey on top and white underneath. This sophisticated coloring makes it difficult to see the shark from above or below. It's camouflaged in perfect ambush colors. Perhaps that's why it's sometimes referred to as a "mugger" of the deep. As with most stealth predators, Jonathan never saw it coming.

The scientific name for the white shark is *Carcharodon carcharias,* and it is the largest predatory shark. Experts say measuring a shark is no simple matter, but they estimate the great white shark can be as long as 20 feet and weigh up to 4,000 pounds, as much as a rhinoceros. It has earned the common name, "great white shark."

One day after lunch, Jonathan was asleep when the phone beside his bed rang. I picked it up quickly, so the ringing wouldn't disturb him. While talking to shark expert John McCosker, I learned that the white shark is a skilled hunter, preying chiefly upon seals, sea lions, fish, squid, and whales and "employing a battery of sensory devices that might rival the detection systems of nuclear submarines."

I learned that the white shark is a complex creature equipped with highly sophisticated senses and hunting skills. Sharks use their senses not only to detect prey, but also to navigate by orienting themselves with the earth's magnetic field and ocean currents. Scientists have shown that white sharks can find prey in the dark, and even when the prey is buried in the sand. It can sense electric signals generated by the muscles of another animal in the water.

"Jonathan's leg muscles were tense and working hard," he explained. "He was kicking hard, and this energy was transmitted through the water as electrical impulses. The muscles of a swimmer can send powerful signals, easily picked up by the shark."

He described the white shark as an efficient and specialized hunter, whose enormous jaws are powerful enough to consume large prey. Although white sharks have been known to attack humans, they prefer the taste of seals.

"When a white shark attacks a surfer, kayaker, or swimmer it's generally a case of mistaken identity," McCosker said. "The outline of a surfer looks like the dark silhouette of a seal against the surface of the water," he explained. "Jonathan was most likely a victim of mistaken identity. Unfortunately, the violence of that initial hit often proves fatal."

Now that we were at a hospital closer to home, friends and neighbors could drop in more often. Our friends called, visited, laughed, and wept tears of joy with us. They called him, "Shark Boy" and "Survivor," and praised him for his presence of mind. Jonathan smiled. Somehow he always managed to keep it light. "I'm not letting anything go to my head," he said, "I still have a lot of work to do to get better. And I'll need lots of help from Mom."

Vicky, our neighbor, was already looking after things at home, delivering food, keeping track of the boys, and offering to help. Our children had grown up together. Playgroup and skinned knees seemed like only yesterday. "You've had more coverage than Clinton," she said to Jonathan.

Michael brought Jonathan a toy beanie baby Shark named, "Crunch." Cecil, one of the mothers from our old playgroup, brought homemade muffins and another Beanie Baby shark. Jonathan's friend, Morgan, brought an even bigger stuffed shark. "Sharks are starting to fill my room," Jonathan laughed.

Susan and her son Alan came with a cold milkshake. Sean and his mom brought flowers and balloons. Jonathan's friend, Jackie, from swim team brought a cuddly, fuzzy toy dog. "It's the opposite of a shark," she said happily. Good cheer, animals, flowers, and cards surrounded his bed.

Jonathan's friend, Peter, and his mom, Nelly, brought a gift of chocolate from Peru, her homeland. "Last year when Peter was rushed to the hospital with a ruptured appendix and nearly died, you and your mom came," Nelly reminded us. "I remember what it's like when your child is in the hospital," Nelly said. "Every mom is very scared. Nothing can compare to the thought of losing a child."

"Now I know how important friends really are, not just for our kids, but for each other," I replied.

Our friend Madeline, one of the moms from swim team joked with Jonathan, "I remember timing you when you swam laps in the pool...I bet you got your best time that day in the ocean, swimming back to shore."

Jonathan laughed and remembered his days of swim team practice in the Lucas Valley pool. "I guess all those laps I swam must have helped."

"Wow, that scar's gonna be a great babe magnet," Debbie remarked, causing Jonathan to blush. "The girls will love it...It's the perfect shape of a shark's jaw."

"Maybe so, but my leg hurts too much to think about that right now," he replied.

Andrew, Tommy, and Greg came with their mom, Marcy. Another strong family of boys from the neighborhood. "Those angels must have been working overtime for you," Marcy said.

"We all prayed for you in church at St. Isabella's today," Marie said when she and her family stopped by on Sunday. "You must have had more than one guardian angel on your shoulder."

"Yes, I think all the angels were there for me," Jonathan replied.

I knew it was true and I believed in angels too.

Leslie came with her son Tristan, our neighbors from Lucas Valley. Tristan had grown up with Jonathan, Michael, and Eric. They were like brothers. "The old neighborhood isn't the same without you...hurry up and get home so you can help us build forts and snake traps," Tristan joked.

"Jonathan, I've known you since you were just a little boy," Leslie said. "You're the most cautious person in the world… how did this ever happen to you, of all people?"

"I guess the shark wanted to know what I tasted like."

"Not very good, I guess, since he spit you out," she laughed.

Kenny, a friend and local surfer, showed up at the hospital not knowing what to expect. He looked at Jonathan covered with stitches and tubes. "My God, Jon," he said. "Are you gonna be okay? I mean your leg…is it still there?"

"Yeah. I still have my leg. And I guess I'm lucky to be alive."

"I was driving home from surfing in Santa Cruz when I heard the news. Everyone's shocked by the shark attack. I can't believe it happened to you, Jon. You're the most careful person I know. You never take chances."

"I still can't believe it myself," Jonathan replied.

"You did a good job, man. You got away. We're all proud of you."

"Thanks. I guess I had to save myself. No one else was going do it for me," he smiled.

"Hey, you got to fly across the bay in helicopter. How cool was that?"

"Painful," Jonathan said, "and I couldn't even see the view. I try not to remember it."

Jonathan's eighth grade counselor from Miller Creek School, Mrs. Brown, head of the conflict resolution team, called to say, "I take full responsibility for teaching Jonathan everything he knew about fighting off that shark in "conflict management." We were grateful for the skills he'd learned.

Marissa came with a big bowl of fresh fruit. She knew how much Jonathan loved fruit, he'd spent many days at her house building water slides and haunted houses with her son, Joseph and enjoying her Italian cooking. "The strawberries are from my garden," she said as she handed the bowl to Jonathan with a fork. It was a gift truly from her heart.

"Thank you, a fresh treat is just what I needed," he said as he devoured the fruit.

"Jonathan your story is amazing…You should write a book. No one else could lead us on a journey like this one," Marissa insisted. "Keep writing…."

We took her advice to heart, writing down our thoughts, fears, hopes, and the milestones in his progress in our journal. My notes were brief — because we were so busy in the hospital — but I wanted to remember all the good news and visitors. Perhaps it was my effort to convince myself that he'd be okay.

Eric drew a series of shark cartoons for Jonathan. Each cartoon depicted talking sharks, sharks who were brothers, and sharks being attacked by humans, with messages from the shark's point of view. "I made these for you," he said proudly, handing them to Jonathan. We smiled at his clever humor, but more importantly I thought perhaps this was Eric's way of expressing and dealing with the fear he felt for his brother.

Many people helped us in countless ways, and many incredible friends were part of the healing. Flowers, phone calls, cookies, candy, cards, and visitors poured into his room. But most of all, their humor and friendship helped us get through each day with its new challenges.

Everyone knew Stinson Beach and everyone wanted to share a part of the experience. Many people told us they were at Stinson Beach that day, or that morning, the week before, or the day after…or they "almost" went to Stinson that day. It became a family joke that EVERYONE must have been at Stinson Beach that day. The stories were endless and amusing. They made us feel connected to everyone in some small measure.

I guess that's why I was surprised to receive a call from someone who really was at the beach that day. "My name is Patricia," she said. "I was at the beach with my video camera. I took the pictures you saw on the news."

"I'd like to hear more about what you saw that day," I said.

"I was at Stinson for my daughter's tenth birthday party. I'd left work early, still wearing my business suit, never expecting to get wet. I was watching the children play in the shallow water when suddenly I heard someone calling for help. I saw Jonathan struggling to shore. I didn't know what happened, but I heard him shouting for help. I sensed something was terribly wrong.

I rushed into the water in my clothes and stockings. By then he'd reached the shore…just sort of floating, hanging on to his board. I could see the water around him turning the color of a faded red umbrella. He was in so much pain, I tried to comfort him.

Within minutes the lifeguard arrived, and he took over. I'm a stringer, a correspondent for a local television news channel, so I grabbed my cell phone to call the station. When I told them what was happening they asked me to film Jonathan on the beach with the video camera I'd brought for my daughter's party. After he was safely on shore, I started filming the scene around him on the beach. My video was shown on the news that night.

As a mother, I thought you'd like to know how brave and calm he was while they tried to get help for him. I don't know how he kept his composure with all the pain, and something as terrifying as a shark. But I thought you should know, you have a very courageous son."

"Thank you for calling to tell me," I said.

"By the way, I noticed two fishing boats anchored close to the beach the day he was attacked. I think there's a connection between the fishing boats and the shark attack."

"Really?" I said. I was surprised to hear this.

"A few years ago I wrote a story for the *San Francisco Chronicle* about fishing boats chumming the water near Bay Area beaches, throwing scraps into the water to attract fish. This brings fish as well as seals and sharks closer to shore, because they follow the food chain. I wanted to publish the story to warn swimmers and surfers that the fishing industry was creating a dangerous situation, drawing predators closer to the beach. My editor refused to print the story because of the local fishing industry's political clout. Finally I dropped the subject and my story was never printed. But Jonathan's shark attack with the fishing boats at the beach confirms my theory."

"I've never heard this before," I said. "Every day we learn something new about the coast."

"Unfortunately, the fishing boat issue has never been well publicized," she said. "Anyway, I still have the video footage from that day, including some footage that was too raw to show on TV, if you'd like to see it sometime."

"Someday," I said.

"Every year on my daughter's birthday, we'll always remember Jonathan and the shark at Stinson Beach."

"We'll think of you on that day, too. Thanks for helping Jonathan." Our lives had become intertwined with another family because of the shark at Stinson Beach.

That afternoon when the phone rang, I put it on the speaker so Jonathan wouldn't have to move.

"Hello, Jonathan," a cheerful voice said. "It's your buddy Logan from Illinois. What were you doing out there swimming with the sharks?"

"Oh, well, it surprised me too."

"Remember those days at the beach in Tower Lakes when things were calm?"

"Logan, you helped me learn to swim, and now look what happened."

"Is it awful?"

"Well, it could be worse. I'm in one piece, and in a good place, but I don't recommend it."

"I'm rooting for you. Get yourself out of there, would you?"

"All right, I will. You take care too."

Jonathan laughed. I loved hearing him laugh. He was beginning to sound like himself again.

The hospital staff accepted the constant commotion of camera crews and a patient who was quickly becoming a celebrity. Jonathan's room was never empty and never lacking excitement.

The NBC crew set up a camera and microphones near his bed. The Dateline interview began right on schedule with many of the questions we'd begun to hear over and over.

"Will you ever go back into the ocean?" It was a question every reporter asked.

"Yes, I hope to…." Indeed it was a tough question and Jonathan's answer was always positive and strong, in spite of the doubts he kept to himself.

"Michael and Eric, what do you think about your brother fighting off a shark?"

"I'm just glad Jonathan got away, and now I want my brother to get strong enough to come home," Eric said.

"If you try to imagine a shark attacking you, to imagine what it was like, to face an animal so big and powerful, you can't even imagine what it was really like...it must have been so terrifying, so overwhelming," Michael said. "And... we know the shark's still out there."

The producer paused for a moment, lost in thought. "Well, I think I've finished my questions for today. I'd like to follow up with you out at Stinson, whenever you're ready to return to the beach."

"I'll try," said Jonathan hopefully.

That night after all the visitors had left, the hospital room seemed so quiet, I was aware of myself breathing, dazed by exhaustion.

"I guess it's true, Mom...God must have other plans for me," Jonathan confided. "I don't know how long my recovery will take or what my life will be like after I leave the hospital. But I want to do something meaningful with my life," he said. "I want to help other people. Not just find a job to make money."

Once again, I remembered the words of my mother. "You'll find your way....Just take it one step at a time."

On the last day of August, I picked up the phone in Jonathan's hospital room.

"Hi Mom, it's Eric. I'm leaving for school in a few minutes. I'm riding my bike today."

"Oh, I'm sorry I'm not there...Did Dad fix breakfast for you and Michael?"

"Yes, he made his famous oatmeal with protein powder...again. It's so thick the spoon stands up in the bowl."

"That's Dad, he's Mr. Efficiency," I reminded him. "At least you won't get hungry," I laughed. "I wish I could be there to wave goodbye on your first day of sixth grade."

"It's okay, Mom. You need to stay with Jonathan."

"I'll see you tonight when you come to visit, and you can tell me all about school." I'd never missed these important events in my children's lives before. But for now, I couldn't do everything for everyone. Reed was there in my place. We all moved ahead with new perspectives on life.

I called Reed at his office. "Just a few reminders.... Eric starts soccer practice after school today. Can you drive him to the field at 4:00?"

"Sure, I've got a million things here, but...sure, I can take some work home. I'll get him there."

"...and Michael has football practice after school until 6:30. Can you meet his bus?"

"Sure, no problem, I'll be there."

"Can you figure out something for dinner for the boys tonight?"

"Sure, don't worry."

"And make sure they do their homework..."

"Okay. Anything else?"

"Yes....Thanks, Reed."

"I'll see you tonight when I bring Michael and Eric over to visit Jonathan."

"Reed...Jonathan's still in a lot of pain...I'm worried...his leg is really swollen...I hope everything's okay."

"Marge, you're worrying too much. Just have faith. He's doing fine. He needs time to heal. He's going to be alright."

"Thanks, Reed, for reminding me to stay positive."

"Despite his brush with death,
Kathrein is confident he will return to the ocean."
- **Maureen, Entertainment News**

Things were moving along, with a few occasional set-backs. Jonathan was afraid to move his leg for fear of worsening his injuries and increasing the pain. I tried to reassure him and focus on the positive.

"Jonathan's progress is amazing," I wrote in our Dream Journal the next morning. "At first, he couldn't move at all. Now, already, he's learning to stand."

"Don't worry, I'll help you," said Sarah, the Occupational Therapist, holding his arm and helping him balance as he stood hesitantly beside the bed. Tubes and bottles hung around him.

At first he trembled visibly. "It's hard work," he said. "I guess I'm weaker than I thought." With the help of Sarah, a full-leg brace, and a walker he could stand until he became lightheaded and had to sit down.

"Tomorrow you'll be strong enough to take a few steps," Sarah replied.

"Good, maybe then I can take a real shower," he said happily.

Reed brought Michael and Eric to visit Jonathan each day after school. His brothers tried to keep him entertained with stories and humor. Maybe they remembered their own childhood fears of ghosts and monsters, fear of the dark, and the fear of climbing down from the highest limb of a tree. They could feel their brother's pain and the frustration of being stuck in the hospital and wanting to be strong again. They, too, saw how quickly life could change.

"Bee stings will seem like nothing after this," Michael joked.

Their presence made a difference and gave Jonathan other things to think about. Eric said his teachers at Miller Creek Middle School called him, "Little Kathrein," because he looked like his two older brothers. Michael said his teachers at St. Ignatius called him, "the forgotten Kathrein," because Jonathan was getting all the attention. But Michael and Eric took the jokes good-naturedly. They were proud of their brother, and proud to be a part of the story.

My job as a mother was to keep life from seeming overwhelming for my children. I tried to hold everything together. My fear was still just below the surface, the fear that someday it would again fall to me to tell those I loved bad news. But my boys kept me on track, reminding me what was important. We still had each other. We're the lucky ones, my mother always said.

Jonathan's wounds were healing, and the pain gradually subsided. Still, he needed our help. I could not leave his side. I slept, or tried to sleep, in the reclining chair beside his bed, listening for his every movement. If pain disturbed his sleep or dreams awakened him, I wanted to be there.

The seriousness had not diminished but, after the fears of the first few days, I was finally starting to believe he was safe. I said silent prayers that he would have the chance to walk and run again.

Now we'd entered the process of healing. The ups and down were endless. I tried to help Jonathan recover from his injuries and at the same time, I tried to recover from my own fears of life and death for my children. We were on a journey together. I knew I could never forget a moment of it. And yet I wondered where it was leading us. We'd taken a huge detour from the route I'd always planned.

He'd always been able to confide in me, and our relationship was especially important now. When I sensed he might doubt himself, I tried to give him encouragement.

"Jonathan, you're an inspiration to so many kids who've read about you and want to meet you. If you'd given up out there in the ocean, or even now, what hope would they have? These kids need you as an example of how to stay strong after a setback in their lives. So many kids look to you as a hero. You're even more than that. You're a role model. Don't worry about what will happen, Jonathan. Just rest and get well."

I saw his eyes brighten. "Yes, I'd like to inspire other kids who face a challenge."

Children stopped by often to meet this new hero. They wanted to see the guy who fought the shark. Their young faces looked at him with such admiration. "What was it like to fight off a shark? Can we have your autograph?" Beneath his name, he drew a shark's fin, his new logo. He was happy to talk to young people and wanted to inspire them. "You can do anything," he'd say, or he'd write, "Always keep trying... *Never give up.*"

> *"I learned to treasure my relationships with others...*
> *My family and friends, and people I*
> *didn't even realize were my friends,*
> *I learned how important other people are in our lives.*
> - Jonathan, CBS 5 Interview

Gradually my confidence improved along with Jonathan's strength. I was beginning to see the beauty of life again. Our journal entry said, "Almost one week since his shark attack... Jonathan is truly my miracle boy."

Each morning after getting the boys off to school, Reed stopped at the hospital on his way to the office.

"Will you be back later this afternoon?" I asked. "With all the questions about Jonathan's condition, you're the one keeping our lives on an even path. I need you. You're the one who keeps me strong."

"Of course I'll be here. I'd rather be here with you and Jonathan than anywhere else. Going to the office is difficult...I can't think about anything but you and Jonathan and our boys."

"Yes, I know it's not easy. I really appreciate everything you're doing for all of us. Thanks for letting me stay here with Jonathan while he needs me."

"I'm going to the office for a few hours ...but I've cancelled all my court appearances and calls. I'll be back as soon as possible."

I looked around the hospital room at the single chair, the disarray of cards, gifts, mementos, and my purse stuffed with notes and papers. This had been my home for days. Nurses knew us and they streamed in and out with food trays, medicine, good wishes, even footies to keep his feet warm.

Never before had I felt so disassociated with *things* in my life and so strongly tied to the people around me. Things didn't matter any more. I was out of touch with the rest of the world. It was impossible for me to concentrate on life outside of Jonathan's world. I'd heard of putting your life in perspective, but this was so abrupt. Unimportant details fell away. We were moving forward, no looking back. Thank goodness we had each other.

Michael and Eric accepted my need to stay with Jonathan. They juggled the demands of school, homework, and sports with visits to the hospital each evening. Maintaining the routine at home was important to their sense of security. Reed was there to give support.

Somehow Reed was able to focus on his work and keep up with things at home, allowing me to give my full attention to Jonathan. He maintained the routine in his own efficient, uncomplicated way. His was a no-frills approach. Each morning he fixed breakfast, packed lunches, and got the boys off to school, tasks that were normally my responsibility.

"Life at home is different without you, Mom...we hope you'll come home soon so we can get back to regular life again." I was glad to know they missed me, but I had no doubt Reed was in control.

Reed remained rock-solid. In spite of his concerns, he encouraged Jonathan and made him laugh. He provided stability just by being there. He questioned the doctors and demanded the best as we moved past the immediate trauma and onto the long road to recovery.

We must be willing to get rid of the life we've planned,
to have the life that is waiting for us.
- Joseph Campbell

"Jonathan, we're going for a walk outside this room today." Sarah stood at the door of his hospital room carrying crutches and a large leather belt.

"Okay, I'm ready for the big excursion," Jonathan replied.

"Don't go too fast or I won't be able to keep up with you," Sarah teased.

"I'm really speedy," Jonathan said with a laugh. I loved his laughter and his optimism. Slowly he lifted himself onto his good leg with the crutches. He walked tentatively down the corridor learning to balance. The muscles were different now. Some had to compensate for others that were gone.

Sarah followed and helped him practice, supporting him with the heavy leather belt she'd strapped to his waist over his hospital gown. I watched him move unsteadily, a few steps at a time and thanked God that he was given the chance to do it. He was learning to walk again and I was joyful at every step.

I held back tears of happiness and called Reed to tell him the good news. "This is silly," I said to Reed. "These days, I seem to weep at everything…even when I'm happy."

"I guess that's because we're so proud of our boys," he replied.

Jonathan inched his way along, moving slowing, tentatively, down the hospital corridor. Any little twist or turn was painful. This moment was indeed the answer to my prayer that Jonathan would walk again.

"Mom, can I please have another drink of water? This is hard work and I'm so thirsty."

I brought the plastic water pitcher with the straw. He leaned on his crutches and I held the water while he drank. He stopped every few steps for more water, and I was happy to help.

"Okay, time to turn around," Sarah said. "You made it past your neighbor's door…That's far enough for today."

"This is a great milestone for you, Jonathan," she said. "You're my best patient."

Jonathan was concentrating on his progress, not worrying about the pain.

Once back to his bed, Jonathan smiled. "That was painful, but worth it." Within minutes he was asleep. I stayed at his bedside and marveled at his accomplishment.

At night, light crept under the door of his hospital room, giving the room an eerie glow. It was unreal, but all too real. I awoke frequently in my chair and looked to Jonathan, sleeping flat on his back, locked in position by the endless rhythm of the CPM machine that moved his leg. The wounds still looked raw, and every movement must have been painful, but seeing him there, asleep next to me, reminded me that he was okay and I tried to relax.

Jonathan improved in strength and spirit. I noticed that whenever he felt stronger, I did too. His energy and confidence were improving, and he was beginning to grow restless, but the doctors weren't ready to let him go. He still had some healing to do and difficulty moving, but Jonathan longed for fresh air and sunshine.

"There's a balcony where we can step outside," I suggested. "Do you think you can you walk to the end of the hallway?"

"I'll give it a try, Mom."

"You can do it, just take your time," I encouraged, as I handed him his crutches.

Jonathan walked slowly on his crutches to a doorway where we stepped out into the sunshine. He stood tall, still holding his crutches. He'd worked hard to reach this milestone. He breathed in the fresh air and together we looked forward to brighter days. He was making progress every day, but to him, recovery seemed slow. He was determined to get well and move on with his life. He couldn't get there fast enough.

Little by little, I began to recognize the gratitude I felt. I reminded myself of our blessings. More than anything, my son was alive. I began to perceive life as a gift and I was thankful each day he improved. Life was presenting us with opportunities to meet people, to appreciate each other, and to grow closer to those we loved. I was in the right place. This was where I needed to be.

I couldn't let myself look upon the shark attack as misfortune. He was getting better and I realized what a blessing we'd been given. Now that he was improving, I was starting to breathe again. He was getting stronger every day and I felt stronger too. Finally I could let go of fear and share my joy with others. I tried to enjoy every moment. Now that Jonathan was safe, I hoped we were back on track.

"Jonathan, you displayed true bravery and real courage.
We are proud of you. You have taught us."
- **Doug Hunt, Jonathan's CYO Basketball Coach**

On Wednesday, September 2nd, eight days after the shark attack, Doctor Toton entered Jonathan's hospital room at 7:00 am with his usual bouncing stride and a smile. For a minute, he just stood at Jonathan's bedside.

"Good morning, Shark Man," the doctor said cheerfully. "Sorry to wake you so early. Today's the day you've been waiting for. I'm here to check you over and send you home."

"Really?" Jonathan's sleepy brown eyes scanned the room, taking in everything that had now become familiar. He closed his eyes again. I was wide awake even though I'd had only a few hours of sleep in the chair. I was excited about this good news, yet wondering about all the details. How this was going to work at all, when Jonathan could hardly walk? And yet the thought of having him home surpassed all other concerns.

The doctor checked him over, and then put his hand on Jonathan's shoulder. "You're outta here young man...You can go home after lunch." These were the words we were waiting to hear.

"Great. I'm ready to go," Jonathan said with the biggest smile I'd seen in days.

Dr. Toton updated Jonathan's prescriptions for pain medications he might need. "We'll need an appointment to take out those stitches," he reminded us.

The doctor discharged Jonathan from the hospital that afternoon, exactly one week after his attack, along with detailed instructions telling us how to care for his physical wounds as well as his emotional scars. Seven days had passed in a rush of details, concerns, and life changes.

Before we left, Kathleen, the hospital social worker, cautioned us about Post Traumatic Stress Syndrome. "The full impact of the shark attack won't be known for some time," she said. "You might see signs even weeks or months from now. Dreams or memories might come back to him un-expectedly." She gave us plenty of reading material to help us recognize the signs that might appear later. "Talking about it is the best therapy," she said.

Reed, Michael, and Eric were on hand, along with Vicky and her daugh-ter, Lindsey, our boys' friend and longtime childhood playmate. The nurses hugged Jonathan and helped him into a wheelchair they'd brought. "We'll miss you...Come back to visit us when you're feeling better."

"Thanks for taking care of me, and for all the good shark jokes."

"Don't forget your teddy bear." Colleen tucked the bear into the wheel-chair next to Jonathan. It was the teddy bear we'd bought for him that first night, that night of great uncertainty.

Twelve year old Lindsey proudly pushed Jonathan's wheelchair through the big doors and out to the curb. A photographer from the newspaper waited just outside the doorway to capture the moment.

"Hold it," he said. "Okay, good, that's it. Your picture will be in the morning paper. Lots of folks around here are following your progress since the day of the shark."

"Really?" Jonathan was still amazed at all the attention.

"Yes, folks want to know if you're okay. And whether it's safe to go back in the water."

"I guess that's the big question," Jonathan said. "I don't have the an-swer to that one."

We lingered with the nurses who stepped outside to say goodbye. Reed brought our familiar white Toyota minivan to the hospital door, with a pil-low he'd placed in the backseat where Jonathan could stretch out his leg. Jonathan climbed into the van, moving carefully. "Please open the win-dows...Let's have lots of fresh air, Mom, it feels so good," he said. I lowered the windows and he settled into his pillow for the ride home.

When we rounded the corner, we were surprised to see the huge banner that hung across the front of our house, "Home of the World Famous Shark Wrestler." The sign was written on a long sheet of white butcher paper, hand-lettered by our neighbor Maggie, signed and decorated with personal messages from the swim team kids, friends, and our neighbors in Lucas Valley.

"Shark Wrestler…Well, I guess that's my new nickname," Jonathan laughed.

We were even more surprised by the group of friends gathered in our driveway, waiting for Jonathan. Kenny, Peter, Bill, David, and Garth cheered when we pulled in, with Jonathan smiling broadly, eager to accept this grand reception. There was a camera crew from the local news too.

"You're our favorite shark fighter," Kenny said, helping Jonathan out of the car.

"I didn't know so many people cared about me," Jonathan admitted in his shy fashion.

We lingered outside in the warm summer evening for a long time, until the sun went down behind Big Rock Ridge and the sky turned golden. Jonathan smiled and leaned on his crutches, surrounded by his friends and happy to be home. Lisa, my dear friend and neighbor, surprised us with a warm dinner and good wishes – somehow she knew we needed help. With so many friends around us, the gathering felt more like a party than a near-death survival. I wondered if this was the end of an experience or the beginning.

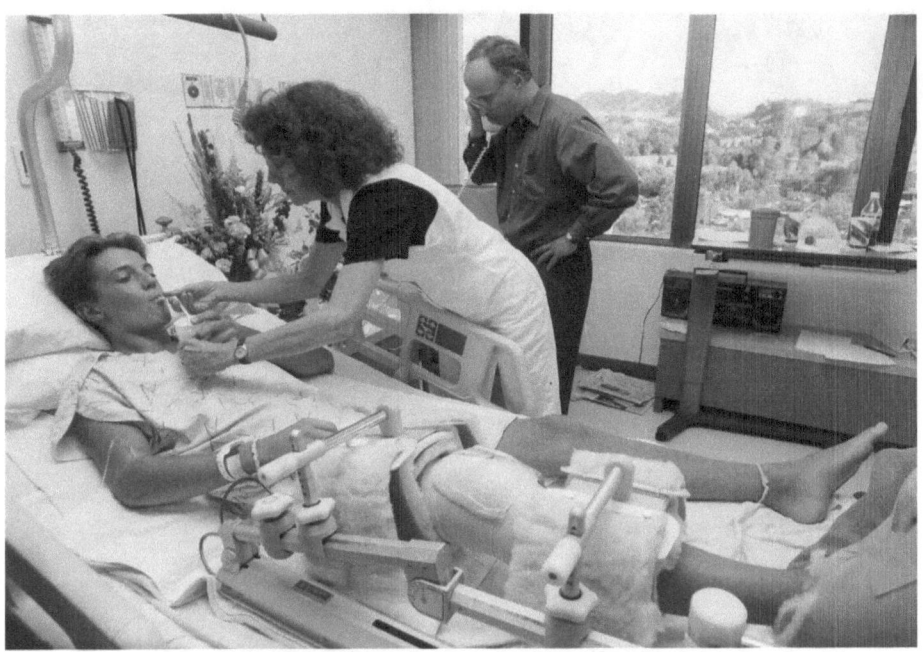

Mom giving a drink to Jonathan who was always so thirsty
after his attack, and Reed on the phone

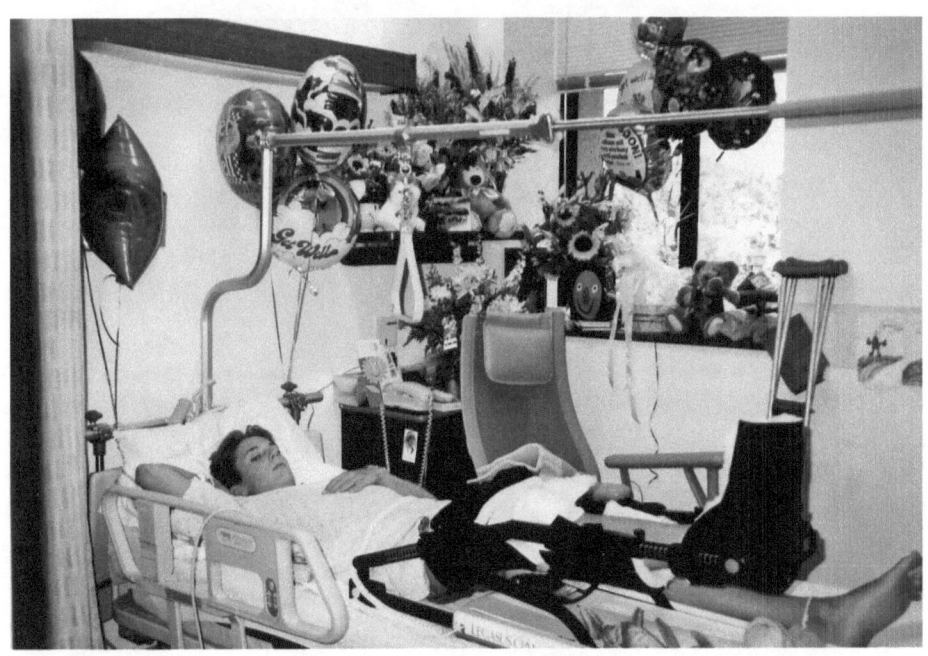

Jonathan with his leg strapped into the CPM (Continuous Passive Motion) Machine

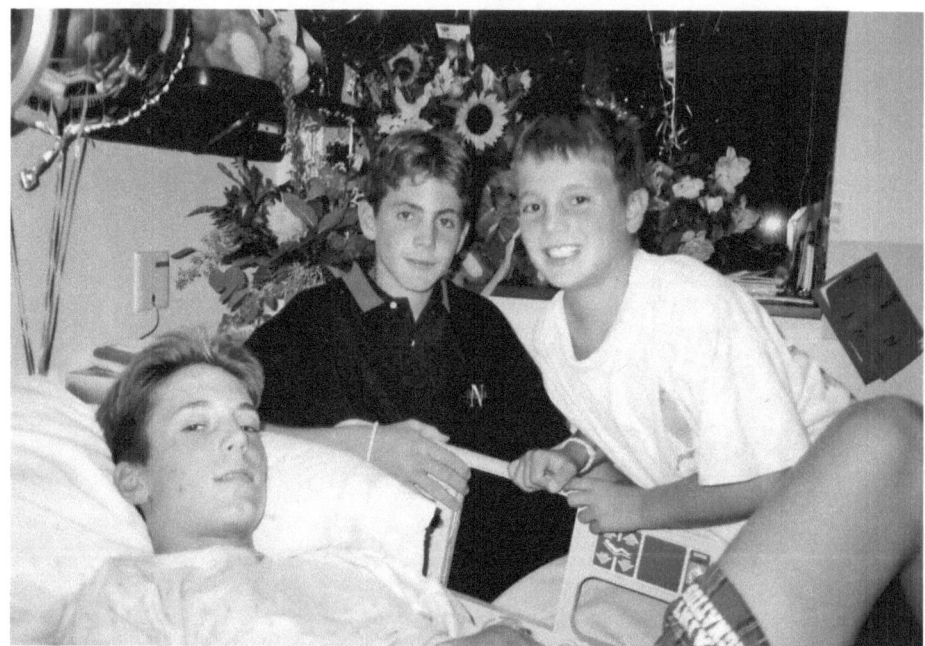

Michael and Eric visiting Jonathan and keeping him company in the hospital

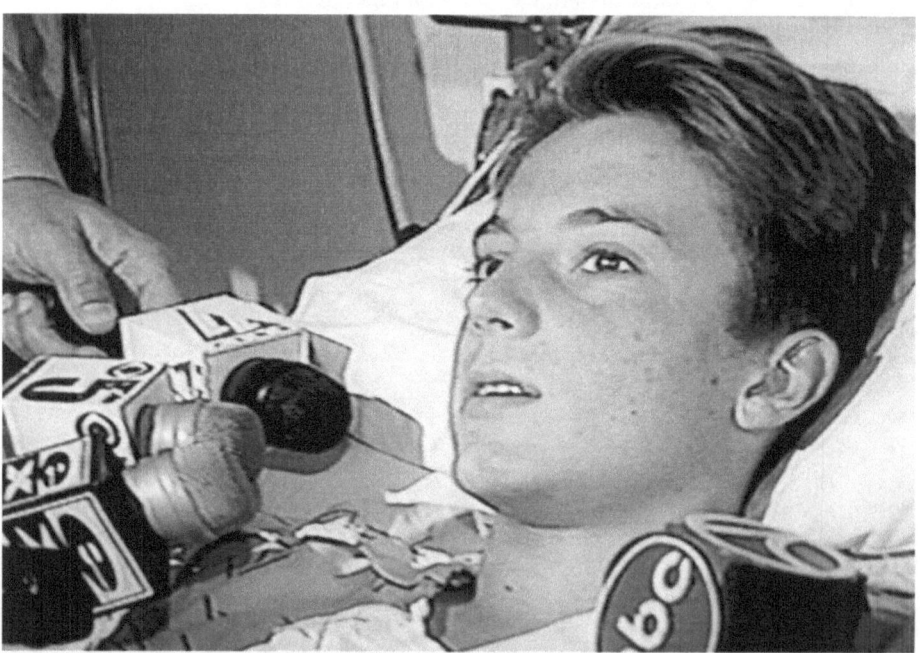

The interview from his hospital bed was like a press conference

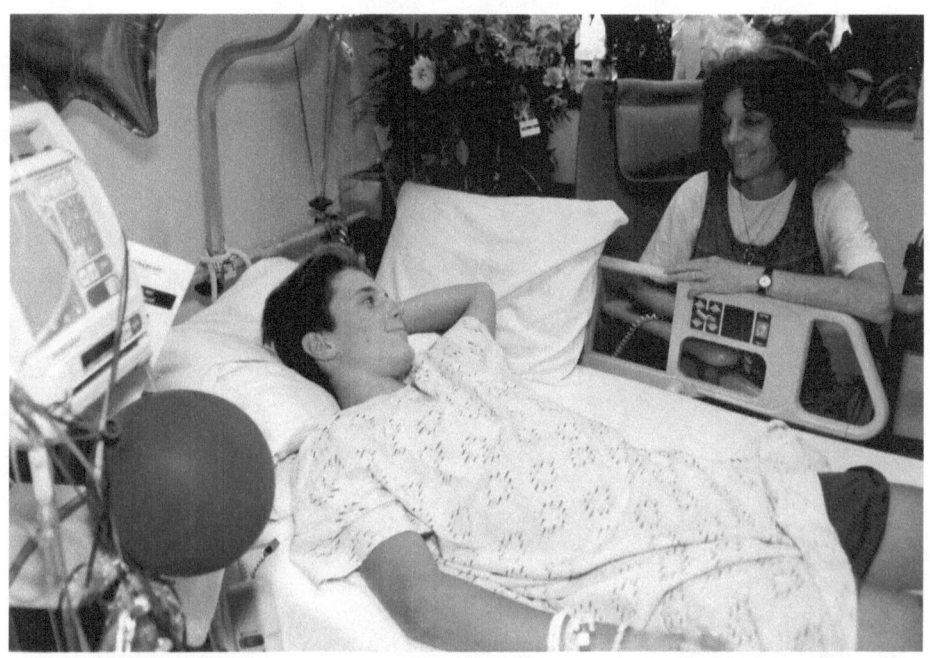

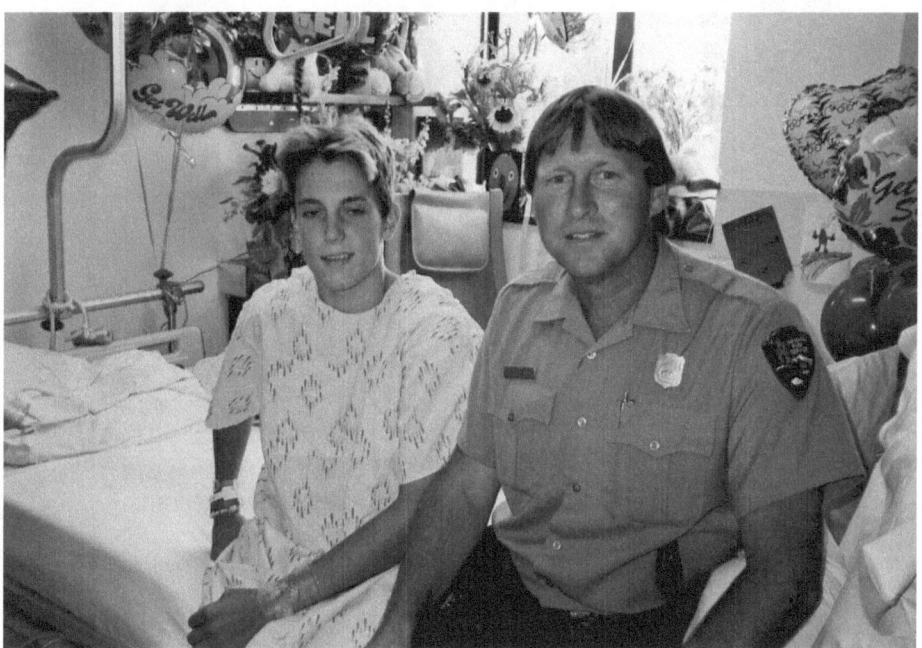

Jonathan and Pat, lifeguard and US Park Ranger, visiting Jonathan at the hospital

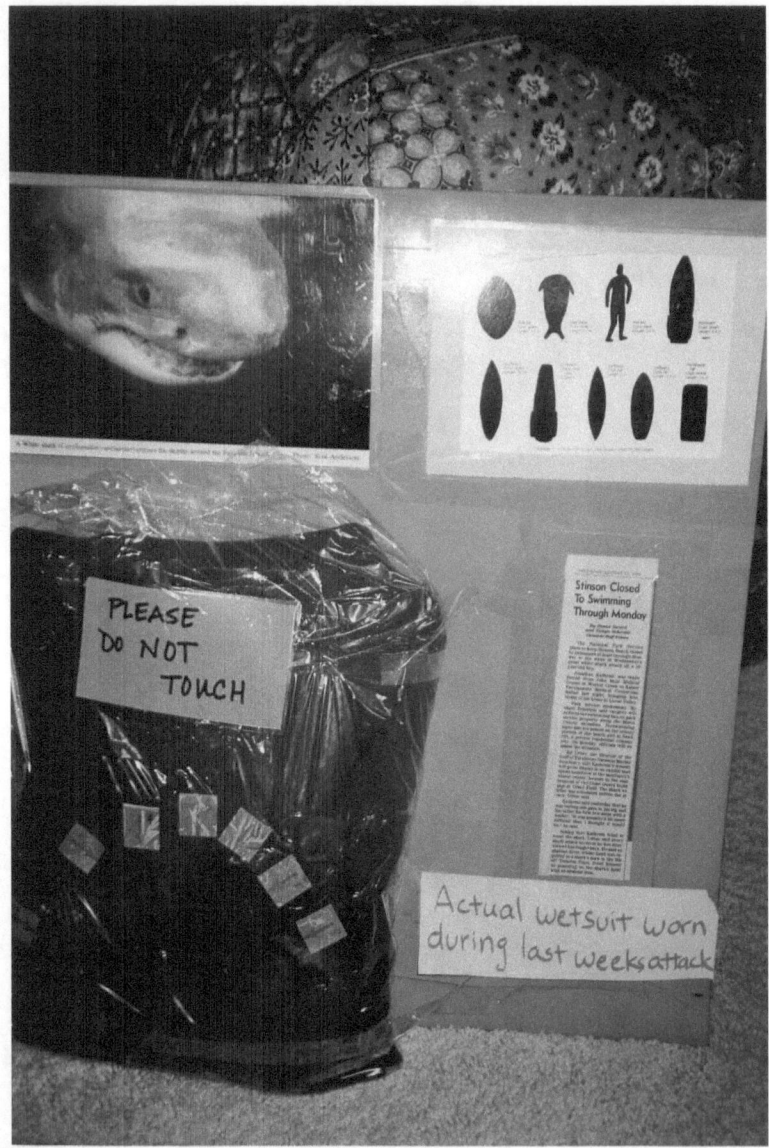

Jonathan's wetsuit mounted for display at Gulf of the Farallones Visitor Center, with arrows marking the shark's teeth marks in the neoprene

Jonathan's swimsuit ripped by the jaws

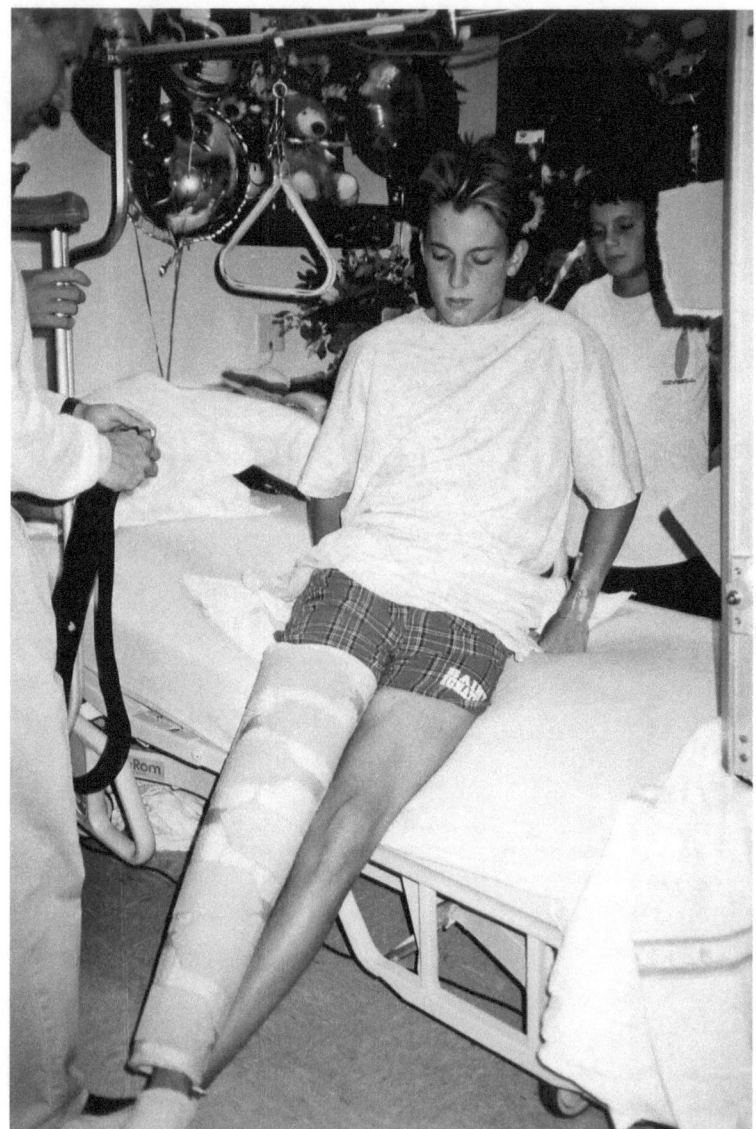

Jonathan learning to walk in the hospital

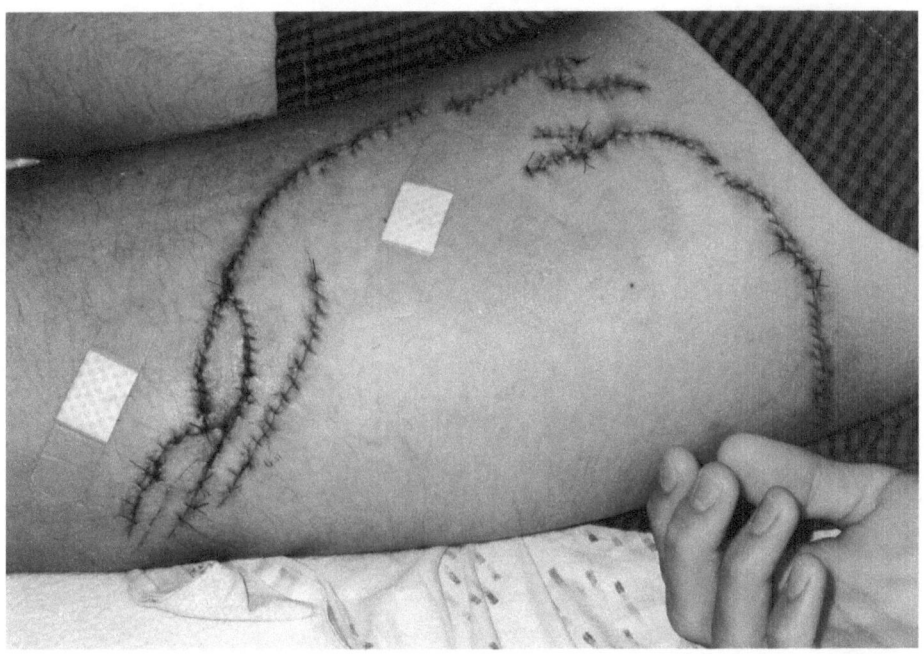

Stitches and scars beginning to heal

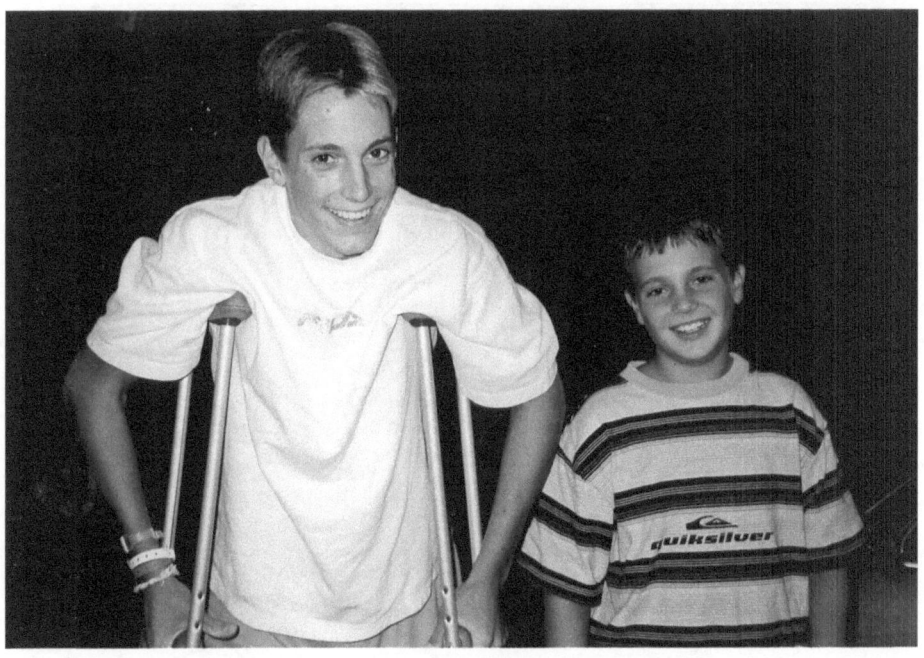

Eric with Jonathan arriving home from the hospital on crutches

The banner that greeted us at home: "Home of the World Famous Shark Wrestler"

Eric's drawing of the shark talking to a Person Expert.

Part Two

Living Beyond the Shark

"For it is one thing to see the land of
peace from a wooded ridge...
Another to tread the road that leads to it."

- St. Augustine

Wednesday, September 2, 1998 – Lucas Valley

I savored the familiar surroundings of home. Even ordinary things seemed different now, more precious than I'd remembered. My perspective had changed during my week in the hospital with Jonathan. I pondered over family photographs, thinking how things might have ended differently. Everything took on new meaning in light of our close call. Knowing how close we'd come to losing our son made me even more thankful to be home. Now Jonathan and I were back on track with Reed, Michael, and Eric and we were a family again.

"Jonathan, how does it feel to be home in Lucas Valley?" Reed asked.

"It's great to be back where I feel safe. I don't think I'll go back to the beach for a long time now that I know what's out there."

We were hardly home when the doorbell and the phone began to ring with calls, messages, and well-wishers. Jonathan was no longer in a hurry to rush off, as most busy teenagers would be. In fact, he couldn't rush off even if he'd wanted to. Instead, when visitors came he wanted to spend time getting to know them, visiting and soaking up friendships he might otherwise have overlooked. Now, people were the most important part of his life, and mine.

I was relieved to be home, but afraid of what our coming home would bring. In the hospital we'd relied on nurses and doctors who were always there, giving him extra attention. I wondered how I could do everything, now Jonathan was totally dependent on me. I helped him move, brought him food, fluffed his pillow, and tried to make him comfortable. I quickly found that helping him gave me great comfort. I could keep him safe. Here he was, my little boy again.

Over the long days and nights in the hospital we'd grown closer. The bond between us that began when he was little had been reinforced and would continue. I was forever changed by my time with Jonathan. His insight helped me see life more clearly. I'd learned about courage, enthusiasm for living, and affection for family and friends.

Left unsaid was my realization that this part of our journey was ending and a new chapter beginning. Most of all, I didn't want our time together to end. Our closeness in the hospital had reassured me. I dreaded, almost as much as I hoped for, the days to come when he would soon be on his own and wouldn't need me at his side. He wanted to get back to school and friends. I wondered how he'd do it all.

Late that night, after everyone else had gone to bed, I sat at his bedside ready to talk - or listen - as we'd often done ever since he was a child in this very room.

"When I close my eyes, I still see the shark," Jonathan confided. "I remember every detail."

"Try not to worry," I said. "It might take some time to put it out of your mind. But you're doing a great job. Think of something positive, like how you'll soon play soccer again."

I stayed with him until he drifted into sleep, not wanting him to be afraid, and wondering if he could ever truly forget.

I checked on all my boys - they were asleep, including Reed. I was comforted knowing everyone was at home and safe. I recalled the hand-lettered banner and the heartwarming presence of many who'd welcomed us home. The outpouring of love was more than I'd expected.

Before going to bed, I wrote in our journal, "Miracles and milestones... we're home at last. Jonathan's homecoming was a joyous event." Now I needed to pick up the pieces of our family routine.

"Hope begins in the dark, the stubborn hope
that if you just show up and try to do the
right thing, the dawn will come. You wait
and watch and work; You don't give up."
- Anne Lamott

Our first morning at home was a joyful, hectic whirlwind that began with my famous sourdough pancakes for breakfast, packing lunches for Michael and Eric, hugging them as they rushed off to school, and then settling down to the tasks of helping Jonathan.

Jonathan's pain ebbed and flowed from manageable to unbearable. His pain and my worries seemed to be synchronized. His wounds were healing, but everything would take some time. Our family routine was shifting. I never knew what to expect.

"Watch carefully for signs of infection," I remembered the doctor's words. "And for signs of post traumatic stress that might appear at any time."

Reed brought in the paper. Headlines blared, *"Marin Coastline is Great White Central."* Just another reminder of the shark in our lives. I was too busy to read the story.

I was the one who was mostly at home while Reed went to work each day and Michael and Eric went to school. After school, Michael went to football workouts and Eric went to soccer practice. Homework, Parish Youth Group, piano lessons, and Indian Guides filled in the empty spaces for Michael and Eric. I considered myself the lucky one to stay at home helping Jonathan and keeping the family schedule running smoothly.

That evening we rented the movie *Sphere* starring Dustin Hoffman. Watching a movie seemed like a good way for us to relax together. We gathered in the family room with Jonathan on the sofa and the rest of us around him. Reed made popcorn and started the movie. Much to our dismay, the predator of the deep bore an uncanny resemblance to a great white shark and tried to eat the main character. The movie turned out to be a complete disaster considering Jonathan's frame of mind and ours. The images were much too real and too much like the one we were trying to forget.

"Okay, enough of this," Reed announced after watching for a while. We hoped Jonathan wasn't too disturbed.

"That was too weird for us right now," Michael said after he turned off the television. We decided to watch *The Wizard of Oz*, instead, which proved to be a better choice.

"Jonathan, you're the lion in this movie," Eric said.

"Why is that? Because my hair's all messy?"

"No, because you had courage all along and you didn't even know it. Just like our family — we're on a journey and we each learn new things along the way."

With Jonathan home, our adventure could continue on a happier path. Our family team was reunited. Helping him recover was a full time job that involved every member of the team. We all did a lot of tip-toeing around, checking, and encouraging.

Jonathan seemed emotionally solid but we didn't know for sure. We encouraged him to continue talking about the attack, not to hold his fears inside. I noticed that he forced himself to look at pictures of sharks in magazines and books. Although it wasn't easy, he was determined to overcome his fear. Even if he might never erase it, he would not let fear dominate his life.

The next day, a blue and white medical supply truck pulled into our driveway. "I'm here to deliver your CPM machine," the young man said as he stood in our doorway. "Where would you like it?"

"Here, on the bed, I guess." I directed him to Jonathan's bedroom. The cumbersome device seemed to take up the entire bed, but Jonathan didn't mind.

"Hey, I read about you in the paper," he said. "I'm a member of the Surfrider Foundation. We try to protect the oceans and clean up beaches for everyone to enjoy. You made big news, taking on that shark... We're all rooting for you." I guess everyone knows Jonathan now, I thought.

"Thanks, keep up the good work protecting oceans and the sharks too," Jonathan smiled.

I helped Jonathan strap his leg into the big device that flexed and straightened his knee. This had become his routine in the hospital and he seemed comforted by it. He used it faithfully and didn't complain. Somehow he even managed to sleep with it because he knew it was important. Ultimately, it provided a kind of security for him. The machine became such a part of our lives that I became accustomed to the constant hum of the motor each night.

Father Tony our friend and Jesuit priest from St. Ignatius high school called on Saturday morning. "I'd like to give Jonathan a sacrament that's reserved for extreme cases." he said.

"Does this mean you think he might die?" I asked. Having been raised a Catholic I was suddenly worried, thinking of "The Last Rites," a sacrament given when death was anticipated.

"No, don't worry. We now call it, "Anointing of the sick." It's meant to give healing and special grace. Jonathan's earned it."

So Father Tony came to our house and we gathered in our living room to share this celebration of life and family. He read from the Bible, "I have fought the good fight. I have run the good race. I have kept the faith." Jonathan, Michael, and Eric liked the sports metaphor. The words seemed to fit our family perfectly and the message gave us a new way to look at our lives.

"I think I can continue the race," Jonathan said. "You've inspired me to keep trying."

"Oh, by the way, here's a key to the faculty elevator," Father Tony said with a smile, handing Jonathan the key. "You'll need this when you come back to school. You've earned it. You'll be the envy of all the kids in the school."

The days following our return home were filled with nonstop activity, calls, visitors, mail, and messages. With so much attention, I had little time to think about myself or what the future would bring. Jonathan answered questions and told his story over and over, often causing visitors to stay longer than they'd planned. Shannon, Joe, and Kate, his classmates from San Francisco came to visit one afternoon and stayed for dinner because they were having so much fun. They entertained him with stories from school and he entertained them with stories of the ocean. The fascination with his shark attack seemed endless.

And yet, Jonathan was still weak and could fall asleep anywhere at a moment's notice. Falling asleep easily was a talent he'd acquired in the hospital and one that continued at home. Sometimes he was so exhausted he slept through everything, even visitors.

Notes came from far and near. Cousins from Iowa wrote, "We're following your story on the Internet...We can't imagine it. Thank God you stayed cool and fought back." Friends from Chicago sent notes, "Now that you're a famous shark wrestler, why don't you retire and take up a less dangerous sport." Children from Dixie School sent crayon drawings of sharks. One child's message said, "I'm sorry you got attacked by a shark. You are a very brave person."

Jonathan had talked to so many shark experts, that Eric decided to draw a shark talking to a person expert. In his cartoon, the shark was saying, "That boy had a strong grip on my gills." Jonathan laughed and hung Eric's drawing next to his bed.

Many of my own concerns were relieved by the steady flow of friends and neighbors who helped in more ways than I could have imagined. Meals and well-wishers appeared at our door. Cecil was my guardian angel, calling, and checking up on me. Vicky often brought dinner, always with her support, encouragement, and humor. I was grateful for their kindness and for my own realization that our friends would accompany us through life no matter what. Amidst all my striving to stay strong and to make the right decisions, friends and family were helping me find the path.

"I feel very lucky to have my leg and my life."
- **Jonathan, SI Genesis Magazine**

Infection remained a concern and intravenous antibiotics continued at the Kaiser Hospital IV Clinic. Some days we made multiple trips for antibiotics and appointments. Fortunately the hospital was only a few miles from our house, but going and coming took a lot of effort and Jonathan moved slowly. With so many appointments, everyone at the hospital knew us. The nurses treated us like family.

The media attention had changed our lives in ways we never anticipated. People recognized Jonathan wherever we went. He was easy to spot with his crutches and his leg brace. Going anywhere with him was like accompanying a superstar. Strangers waved and stopped to shake his hand and congratulate him. People even congratulated me too, for raising such a level-headed kid, but I attributed it all to him.

By Friday, September 4th he was making progress, but everything still hurt. That afternoon, when I took him to Kaiser for his appointment, the doctor said, "Not surprising that your leg still hurts...These wounds are deep and you're still healing."

Kelly, the nurse, patiently spent an hour snipping and pulling out every one of the tiny black threads. Jonathan's stitches were finally out - another milestone. "Everything looks good," the doctor said. "Keep massaging the scars to break down that scar tissue."

Jonathan was on the mend. His healing wounds were symbols of the strength he'd gained on the inside too. We'd been fortunate in this journey that began on the day of the shark, not so very long ago. How could I ever thank God for all the good news that might have been bad news?

As a family, we took each day as an opportunity to help him recover in body and spirit. We supported and encouraged, and tried to keep his spirits up. And yet, in private Reed and I found questions lingering in our minds. We didn't know if he would ever walk without a limp, or run to catch a football with his brothers. We wondered about the long term psychological effects yet unknown.

> *"It's a big wilderness,*
> *and there are wild animals out there."*
> **- Golden Gate National Recreation**
> **Area Spokeswoman**

Wednesday, September 9, 1998 marked the two week anniversary of Jonathan's attack. It had been an incredibly tense two weeks. I'd hardly slept and we were all on edge, worrying. Jonathan was healing but I still couldn't relax until he was out of danger. Our lives had been thrown upside-down and everything had happened so quickly. The day of the shark still seemed like yesterday.

We drove to the John Muir Medical Center in Walnut Creek for follow-up appointments with his trauma surgeons. Seeing the hospital again, I remembered all the uncertainty of that first day. In spite of my anxiety, I tried to be cheerful and focus on how far we'd come. The doctors were going to see if everything was okay. And what if it wasn't?

Dr. Attaran removed the strips of steri-tape that protected his wounds. "His scars look good, and everything's healing well," he said as he observed the results of his meticulous work. He'd done a remarkable job repairing Jonathan's leg with so many delicate stitches.

"Thank you for helping Jonathan," I said. "You made a big difference."

Next, Dr. Davis took x-rays of Jonathan's right knee. "Your knee is tracking perfectly, and looks like it's working well so far," he said. "Soon you should have full use again."

"When can I start to exercise?" Jonathan asked.

"You're ready to go, young man." Jonathan was happy to hear this good news. I was thankful and relieved that Jonathan was so eager to push ahead.

That evening he took the luxury of his first real bath. And he could bend his leg enough to put on his pajamas. "I'm getting back to being strong again," Jonathan said. I was proud of his optimism, but I could see more hard work ahead.

The next day when I awoke, I realized we'd reached a new level…he had taken only one pain pill that night…and he'd awakened only twice during the night. Jonathan was getting better and his pain was more manageable. He was sleeping better. I could sleep too. Each day and night was better than the one before. I was thankful things seemed to be going well so far, but he still had lots of healing to do.

The next day, Thursday, September 10, 1998 was Eric's eleventh birthday. We celebrated his birthday and Jonathan's progress. It was an important day for brothers to share their happiness. When we gathered around to light the candles on Eric's birthday cake, I noticed how the glowing candles illuminated the faces of all three of our boys and life seemed good after all.

That night, Jonathan turned over in bed for the first time since his attack. His independence was returning. "It wasn't easy, but I did it," he said. He was proud, and I was happy to note another step along this road with a destination still unknown.

> *"I know you were spared for good*
> *things in life yet to come…*
> *Recognize them when they come your way."*
> - **Grandma McClellan**

Michael ran to answer the door on Friday afternoon. "Mom, you won't believe this…Grandma's here," he called to me. Eric and Michael rushed to give her hugs.

I sank into her arms. Here was my team-leader.

"Mother...what a surprise."

"Families have to stick together ... a little moral support never hurts." I'd heard her say these words many times before, but I'd never felt their meaning as much as now.

"I'm so glad you're here," I said, trying to hide my disbelief. "I could really use your support."

She leaned down to give Jonathan a hug as he sat on the sofa with his leg outstretched.

"I brought a few little gifts for the boys," she said, pulling out games and puzzles and surprises. She was a real life Auntie Mame, filling the house with laughter. She always seemed able to see the world through their young eyes.

I welcomed her presence and most of all, her reassurance. She was my role model and my inspiration. I was still her little one, just as Jonathan was my little one. Her presence comforted me in a way no one else could. She was the perfect mother, always there when I needed her. It was her family tradition to be there whenever needed, or whenever she thought she could help, and now I knew how important that was.

"Get out the cards," she said. "Let's have a game of King's Corners."

"Okay, I'll deal," said Michael, as he and Eric took their favorite spots, sitting on the floor around the coffee table.

"Tonight I'll bake an apple pie because you've been so good, and because it's your dad's favorite." Everyone got special attention when Grandma was around.

She helped pass the time for Jonathan by telling stories of her childhood, life during the Great Depression, and her days of teaching music to children in school. Together we reminisced about family gatherings. In the Midwest we called it visiting....family and friends talking in that relaxed stream of consciousness about comforting subjects like the weather, relatives, and the funny things neighbors do. Visiting brought us closer to each other. And in some ways, things hadn't changed. Jonathan's experience would someday be his story for his grandchildren.

Grandma and Jonathan sat together for hours. She massaged his scars with great care as the doctors had instructed, to help his wounds heal. I remembered from my own childhood how healing her touch could be. Her undivided attention was priceless in so many ways.

"Jonathan, when your mom was a little girl, I used to sing to her if something was bothering her. *"There was a little bird, built a nest in a tree... and laid little eggs in it one two and three...."* Her familiar voice was the most beautiful sound I'd heard in ages, and brought tears to my eyes. I knew the song and all the verses.

"That was a sad song, Grandma. But it helped me realize things aren't so bad after all."

"That's the point of a sad song," she said, smiling.

"And Margie dear, what about you?" She turned her attention to me. My familiar nickname reminded me again of my childhood when she was always there for me. Now the paths of our lives were crossing once again.

"I'm concerned you're keeping everything inside. Are you doing okay?"

"Mother, I've been watching you all my life. You're my role model for how to deal with tough times. I've learned from you that it's important to accept, and take things one step at a time." I remembered when my father died, as difficult as it was for my mother, she often repeated the words, "I accept."

"Margie, I'm proud of you. You're doing a good job helping your boys... and keeping your perspective too." I felt her pride in me that had always been so important to me as a child.

"Thanks, Mother. It's important for you to be proud of me, at any age."

The coming days continued to be challenging for Jonathan and for all of us. He practiced walking and moving toward each new goal - to give up his crutches, to walk with only the leg brace, to be strong enough to run. Our entire family pitched in to help. We encouraged him to continue his progress and not give up. Michael and Eric were his legs, offering to bring whatever he might need. They knew he might have scary memories, and they were very comforting. We were our own village, ready to help each other.

On Sunday, September 13, he tried a few steps without crutches. Each movement was careful and cautious, in the safety of our kitchen. Another miracle, I thought. He'd accomplished his biggest goal yet - his first real steps.

"At first I didn't know if my leg would hold, but it did." We cheered and shared his joy.

"I should write this in your baby book right next to the day you took your first baby steps." To me, this milestone was even more remarkable because of his struggle to get here.

"I'm proud of you, Jonathan, for all your hard work to get better," I said, remembering how important a parent's pride could be.

The next day Jonathan took off the brace...he could lift his leg and move it forward while sitting...something he couldn't have done four days earlier at Dr. Davis' office. Seeing his progress helped him move forward.

"No piano lessons for Michael and Eric today," I'd written on my calendar. At least for now, some things had to go.

"Today is the first day Jonathan hasn't been on the front page of the newspaper...Why not?" Vicky asked, half joking – half serious, as she appeared at our door for one of her frequent visits.

"I guess I'm no longer front page news," Jonathan laughed. We were ready to let the media attention fade away.

My mother returned to Wisconsin on Sunday September 20th. I'd depended on her cheerfulness and encouragement during her visit. Now the pressure was on me to keep everything together. Suddenly I was on my own again, helping Jonathan along with the hectic schedule of a busy family of boys.

"You'll do just fine," she said as she left. Thanks to her endless encouragement, I believed her. But I felt a great emptiness without her cheerful presence. I called her every day to report on Jonathan's progress and to receive her moral support.

Michael carried home armloads of textbooks for Jonathan with assignments and messages from his teachers. Most days Jonathan was too tired even to look at them. He couldn't focus on schoolwork. His thoughts were occupied with sharks, doctors, and trying to heal.

Vicky continued to check on me. She could see that I was overwhelmed. She brought food, and love, and offered to listen. She made sure I had fresh vegetables from the farmer's market, and most of all, a best friend.

She was my sounding board, the one who helped me sort out my emotions. She was my first friend when we moved to California, and someone I'd always relied on in so many ways. We'd been through a lot together, raising our kids, and we weren't finished yet. I realized that friends are friends for all kinds of reasons, and I never really knew how important a friend could be until I needed one.

Jonathan returned to school on Monday, September 21st, four weeks after the attack. For most kids, school was just part of the routine. But for Jonathan, getting back to school was an achievement, one of his happiest days. He was back where he belonged.

Getting there was tiring and, at times, painful. He wore a sturdy leg immobilizer with a metal frame. He couldn't drive so his friend Phil met us at Starbucks each morning to give him a ride. Jonathan couldn't bend his leg, so he inched his way into the backseat and sat sideways for the ride to San Francisco. I wondered what his thoughts would be, looking out at the great ocean as he crossed the Golden Gate Bridge.

I dropped him off and waved goodbye, thankful for friends like Phil who could help. It was difficult for me to see him go, especially after all the togetherness we'd shared. I wanted to always be important in his life and didn't want to lose the bond we'd developed.

After school, he was eager to tell me about the excitement of his return. "Mom, I got a huge welcome. They played the theme song from *Jaws* and all the kids cheered when I walked into the gym. I never knew so many other kids cared about me."

"At first your shark attack was a shocking event in our lives," I said, "and now it's helped us learn so much about other people." Getting back to his friends and activities was another step in the right direction.

"The kids surrounded me in the hallway asking me to tell the story again and again. My friends call me, 'Shark Bait' and 'Shark Man.' My friend Matt said, 'You must not taste very good or the shark would have finished you off...' I realize now how many friends I have."

"I can tell you're happy to be back at school where you can laugh about it," I observed.

With everyone at school, the house was quiet. I had more time for reflection. The past four weeks had brought much happiness as well as many new concerns. Now, whenever my boys left home, I was aware of the unspoken possibilities. Every time I waved goodbye, I thought of Jonathan that day he left for the beach. I couldn't erase the fear of the phone call I remembered so well. I still felt a lingering insecurity.

When Michael and Eric left for school each day, saying goodbye took on new meaning. Hugs and kisses became more important. Even my mother had noticed, "No one ever comes or goes from this house without a hug."

Each time they returned, I wanted to be there to hear about the goal Eric scored in soccer practice, or the football pass Michael caught on the ten yard line. I needed to reconnect with their lives too.

Jonathan propelled himself into the demanding work of healing, physical therapy, and school. Everything required his full effort. An exercise bike was delivered to our house but most days after school he was too tired to use it. He simply fell asleep.

With Jonathan gone, I was suddenly alone. I was unprepared for our abrupt separation and the void I would feel. Even though he was away for only a few hours each day, I missed him terribly. I knew his independence was an important part of healing. While he was moving ahead, I was suddenly on my own, trying to catch up with my life.

Our lives moved into their separate orbits, and once again we fell into a rhythm. Each morning I'd get the boys off to school, giving Jonathan any special help he might need. Each afternoon I'd coordinate sports and other activities, trying to keep our lives balanced and involved. My priorities were with my family even more than before. I wanted to be there for each one of them.

Outwardly, Jonathan didn't seem rattled by his experience, but getting around was difficult, and the shark was not easily forgotten. Recovery was hard work and painfully slow. He still walked with a limp, unable to run or swim. He needed a support team and our family was the team. His recovery became a commitment for all of us. Family backing was critical and our love was the most important element we could provide. He wanted to be as strong as before, and we wanted to help him get there. Each day was a progression toward that goal.

The relationships I'd nurtured in my boys over the years had become invaluable. Everything now made sense. Brothers were there when you needed them. Brothers were best friends. Without realizing it, perhaps this was why I'd found it so fulfilling to stay at home and be a mom all those years. The lessons now had real meaning. I'd been preparing for this journey too.

I watched my boys together. "They've all grown up so fast," I said to Reed. "Now they've seen the reality of how quickly life can change."

"They've built on everything we've taught them over the years, and the lessons have brought them closer, not just as brothers but as friends," Reed said.

> *"I'm an athlete, but I don't have a sport*
> *right now," Jonathan said.*
> *"Yes . . . but you've got your life."*
> - Frank, CBS News

September to December, 1998

By the end of September we realized that routine physical therapy was not aggressive enough for Jonathan. He was determined to become an athlete again. Our friend, Kathy, told us about "Active Care," a sports medicine facility in San Francisco where professional athletes trained after injuries. When we saw Jerry Rice of the 49ers, one of the greatest wide receivers in NFL history, and Natalie Coughlin, a Cal swimmer and future Olympic gold medal winner, as well as all the latest equipment and monitors, we knew this was a place for recovery.

One athlete noticed Jonathan's ragged scar and teased him, "Where did you have your knee surgery done... Bosnia?" We laughed, but in fact, Jonathan was proud of his uneven, jagged scar. It was a sign of the close call he'd survived.

I realized how scars have the mysterious ability to remind us of the stories of our lives, the stories that become our family history. Jonathan's scar dominated his leg, and was the source of many questions and stories. It would always be a reminder of this path we had not expected to follow, and the joys we'd found along the way.

Jonathan began his new exercise regimen in earnest. I drove him to regular sessions in San Francisco where Coleman, his physical therapist, taught him how to strengthen weak muscles and how to compensate for ones that were missing. He encouraged Jonathan not to be afraid to push his strength to new limits. Jonathan was ready for hard work, but it wasn't easy. After each session, he wrapped his leg in ice and slept all the way home.

While he worked on getting stronger, I walked to the majestic St. Ignatius Church at the top of the hill overlooking the city of San Francisco. Each time I entered this silent world of soft light filtered through stained glass, I lit a candle and said a prayer for Jonathan and for all of us. As I kneeled and prayed, the flickering candles reminded me of my childhood when the world seemed safe. I remembered how fortunate I was to have my son.

With his new physical therapy program, Jonathan improved immediately. I noticed he moved less tentatively and became more clear about his goals. I saw new confidence emerging.

"I'd like to get back to my soccer team. And maybe start swimming again too." And he began to talk more seriously about returning to the ocean to surf. "I think I could do it, Mom, my leg's getting strong enough."

"But why?" I asked.

"It's something I need to do, for myself. I really miss the ocean."

"Let's think about it," I suggested.

"Miracles can happen...You're living proof!"
- **Aunt Bev and Uncle Larry**

On October 18, 1998, a balmy Sunday afternoon, we hosted a backyard Victory Party to celebrate Jonathan's escape from the shark and to thank our friends who'd supported us. Our yard was filled with balloons and happy families. Jonathan wore a bright orange shirt, an optimistic color he said. Together we basked in the glow of his victory as the sun set over Lucas Valley.

One day later, Jonathan and I took a long walk along the fire trail in the hills. From the path above our house we looked down upon Lucas Valley, admiring the beauty, detached from the cares of his ordeal. Jonathan paused to touch and admire every little plant and flower along the way, taking in all of nature, as I silently acknowledged the miracle of his survival. Since the day of the shark, his life had detoured down a different path, more demanding than any I could have imagined. He had come to understand the ocean, the great white shark, and the ways that life could change so unexpectedly. Indeed, his world view, and mine, had changed.

The next day, Jonathan broke out with poison oak, but he handled it good-naturedly. To him, this was only a small set-back compared to everything else. "Mom, it was worth it to be outside, walking with you in the hills again."

The press continued to call and come to our house for follow-up stories about the attack and the seeming prevalence of sharks at Stinson Beach. Most of the time, Jonathan was happy to accommodate their requests. He accepted most interviews that didn't interfere with his recovery, school, or physical therapy. Because of the ongoing interest in his story, he didn't need to hold anything inside. Reed and I believed that talking was good therapy and the interviews seemed to help him gain confidence.

During every interview, Jonathan reflected on his experience and spoke from his heart. His words were vivid and unrehearsed, revealing his fears as well as his fascinations. "As a kid, I had these images of a sea monster coming up and grabbing me when the water was too murky. I was especially scared when I was waterskiing… every time you fall you're sitting, waiting for the boat to circle back around, it's the feeling that something could just swim up underneath you. I had really just gotten over that fear when I was attacked by the shark out at Stinson Beach."

His words surprised me, because over the years he'd always seemed so comfortable in the water. I listened as he continued.

"Now I realize there was probably a good reason why I was afraid of being attacked by something in the water."

Sometimes the reporters wanted to hear my point of view as a mother. Putting my thoughts into words helped me to recognize the blessings in our story. I gradually came to realize that the media, with its constant interest, was providing an outlet for me too. Talking about Jonathan's bravery and how we'd survived as a family had become my safety valve too.

The Red Triangle continued to be a headline topic in the local newspapers, with maps and articles outlining this infamous shark zone. As a result of Jonathan's attack, the area became known as, "Shark Central." And Stinson Beach, so close to home, was in the heart of the triangle.

We accumulated a collection of gifts from reporters and TV news channels - coffee mugs, miniature TV trucks, NFL Film sweatshirts, T-shirts, Sports Illustrated caps, Dateline caps, pencils, pens, and video tapes of his interviews. At times our home looked like a film studio with news crews, lights, cameras, reflectors, and news vans with satellite dishes parked in the driveway.

Each interview became a big production with equipment, set-up time, questions for Jonathan, and reporters rushing to make the five o'clock news. Interviews often took longer than expected because reporters became personally engrossed in his story and wanted to continue talking to Jonathan and asking questions.

At first we didn't mind the media intrusion into our lives because the shark had turned things upside down anyway. But we soon began to recognize the extent of the media's influence. Many times dinner was delayed by a news crew in our living room filming an interview. Our schedules were disrupted by delays and last minute requests. Even after the cameras stopped rolling, the crew often stayed to talk. The phone rang constantly with more requests. The novelty was wearing thin. He'd answered the same questions over and over. As a family, we were starting to resent the inconvenience of this encroachment in our lives.

Our need for privacy became a real issue. Jonathan was proud of his survival and willing to tell his story, but the time spent talking to the press became overwhelming. Facts were frequently misquoted, with little reliable information about sharks, no follow up, and hardly even a thank you to Jonathan or our family for the inconvenience.

> *"My experience has stayed with me*
> *and changed my ideas."*
> - Jonathan Kathrein

Awareness of sharks off the coast of San Francisco had increased and the local media was eager to capture the public interest with headlines. Reporters pressed for sensational details, but Jonathan refused. He never talked about sharks as killers or reinforced the *Jaws* stereotype.

"I think it's pretty clear that sharks are not trying to eat people," he said. "A shark can eat you if it wants to, there's no question about that… I know from my experience that if that shark wanted to eat me, it would have…but when the shark discovered that I wasn't a seal, it let me go."

Jonathan preferred to focus on information he'd learned about how important sharks are to our environment. He wanted people to understand the shark, not blame it.

"I'd like others to learn from my experience. I want programs that might help another person who faces a shark. And valid information that helps people understand sharks."

We soon leaned the press did not share his desire to provide scientific information with educational value. In most cases, their goal was only to provide entertainment and sensationalism. Jonathan began to decline interviews that were not in some way educational or scientific. As a result, his interviews became less frequent and life at home became quieter.

By late fall of 1998, my emotions had become as unpredictable as the ocean. One minute I was confident and bursting with pride that Jonathan had saved himself from the jaws of a shark. The next moment an unexpected melancholy took its place. At first I'd been relieved and thrilled by his survival, but my euphoria soon faded. I recognized the complexities of such a close call and I didn't know whether to feel happy or scared. My happiness was overshadowed with guilt and other worries, along with the mundane routine of trying to get life back to normal.

I blamed myself. I'd gone over it in my mind hundreds of times. If only I'd been there. I could have done something. I should have been with him on the beach to help and comfort him. Maybe I shouldn't have let him go to the beach on his own. If only I'd said no. He was only sixteen, hardly ready to face the world alone, and I'd let this happen. I couldn't erase my feelings of guilt. If only I'd done something.

The shark attack had made the world seem overwhelming. Other details of life seemed so trivial now that we'd survived the greatest scare of our lives. I was sad that life could be so unexplainable and overwhelming.

The ocean had let us know just how small we really were and the experience had made me feel vulnerable.

My emotions were fragile. I cried at unexpected moments – out of relief, thankfulness, fear, but mostly I didn't know why. Sometimes, mostly when I was alone and reflecting on what had happened, tears spilled out and left me feeling helpless. When I least expected it, I was in pieces again. While Jonathan moved ahead, I was entangled in the fears of how close we'd come to an even greater tragedy. Outwardly, I tried to appear optimistic. I kept my feelings inside so my family and friends wouldn't notice. I tried to be strong for those who depended on me, but inside I felt powerless. I was in a constant state of anxiety and worry. Unexpected things could happen. On top of everything else, I was feeling sorry for myself, regretful that this should have happened to my Jonathan.

Even though the urgency of the attack had subsided, I couldn't get my head to clear. The trauma was difficult for me to forget. Why did this happen to my child? Some of my friends had experienced trouble or crises with their children, and I wondered if they'd felt this way too.

Jonathan's outlook seemed more confident than my own as he engaged in the challenges of recovery. Outwardly, he appeared undaunted by the near-death experience, and yet he admitted he was afraid the shark would take his life. I was certain that the fear remained with him, but he chose not to dwell on it.

School was demanding. He was tired and distracted by the difficulties of maneuvering just to get around. Constant pain in his knee made getting through each day an ordeal. Ongoing rehabilitation sapped much of his energy. He couldn't concentrate on his schoolwork. He found the subjects at school so remote from his recent life and death experience that he had difficulty focusing. Most days he came home and fell asleep, too exhausted to attempt his homework. The demands of physical therapy were paramount, and schoolwork had to slide.

I was on the phone with teachers and counselors trying to intervene. He'd missed so much; I hoped he wouldn't lose a semester. Fortunately, his teachers accommodated his needs and Jonathan pushed ahead.

Jonathan had become too busy for interviews and calls from the press were less frequent. I was relieved we were no longer in the spotlight. Our days were quieter with fewer intrusions. Life had become more peaceful and less complicated for me but my days were lacking purpose. With Jonathan on his own, the return to normalcy brought a new emptiness. Days at home were too quiet after the flurry of the preceding weeks. With all three of my boys at school, the days grew long and the house seemed empty. I was beginning to feel the emotional fallout that accompanied the sudden injury to someone I loved.

When I came across childhood photos of Jonathan around the house, I thought about how close we'd come to losing him and how things might have turned out differently. I was sentimental about everything, and my tears were never far from the surface.

Over the coming weeks, I worried whenever he left my side. For me, every situation was loaded with what might happen. His return to school and his activities brought new concerns. What about his scars? The torn muscles? His knee? What about the traffic on the way to school?

One morning I received a call from the school office. Jonathan was involved in a fender-bender on the way to school, in a car filled with kids and one of his friends driving. Fortunately everyone was fine, although a bit shaken, and the call reminded me that anything could happen.

I'd become frightened of life. I'd seen how easily unexpected things could happen. Life seemed fragile. I saw a dangerous world. Even the ocean I'd always loved seemed treacherous. I wanted to keep my boys safe. Fortunately they had no desire to enter the ocean, at least not right away. I'd forgotten my own love of the ocean and how uplifting it had always been for me. For me, the ocean was now something to fear, but difficult to ignore because it was so close.

I felt different from everyone else. None of the other mothers I knew worried about sharks or life and death struggles. They weren't afraid of the message they might hear the next time they answered the phone. No one really understood how upsetting this trauma had been for me. I couldn't forget the fear of nearly losing a child. I was in a world of my own, drifting, isolated and apart from everyone around me.

I wrestled with my own emotions every day. My moods varied from exuberant to anxious and depressed. I couldn't shake the memories, or the fear of losing him, and I was frequently reminded of this traumatic event whenever I heard Jonathan telling about his attack. Nothing had ever touched me so deeply.

Without realizing it, I was suffering the symptoms of post traumatic stress. I didn't recognize this as part of the healing process. The shark attack had affected me in so many ways...I needed to weave these threads together to find new meaning. Right now the threads of my life were barely connecting.

"One can make a day of any size
And regulate the rising and setting of his own sun
And the brightness of its star."

- John Muir

I sought solace with Father Keane, our priest and family friend. I was searching for meaning. He reminded me that sudden tragedies are sometimes meant to test us. "You can't prepare for something like this," he said, "and you can't compare it to anyone else's experience. A crisis can affect us in positive or negative ways," he said. "You must decide how to respond."

"This experience is uniquely my own, that's what makes it so difficult. I don't know anyone else who's ever had to decide how to respond to a shark attack in their family," I said.

"But in many ways your experience is similar to urgent situations faced by other parents. The lessons are universal. You're a mother and your first thought is to help your injured child. But you need to keep yourself strong too. You set the example for your family. You're trying to raise children who can cope with life and not fall apart. That's the goal."

He was exactly right. For months, I'd spent my energy giving Jonathan support and helping him focus on his recovery so he wouldn't get discouraged. But I'd neglected myself.

Father Keane's advice was simple, and yet it helped tremendously. I needed to be strong for my family and for myself. I couldn't neglect myself or my feelings, and I was not alone in the journey. For me, this understanding was a journey back to healing.

Ultimately, my family was most important to me. My mother had always been my guiding hand, and now I needed to guide. Support for each other was the simple but important lesson I wanted to impart to my children. I needed to be strong for myself and for them. With this goal in mind, I was ready to carry on.

I realized that amidst all the commotion and attention surrounding Jonathan, my relationship with Reed had suffered too. I'd shuffled our relationship into the background, giving Jonathan top priority. Inadvertently, I'd neglected us. Over the recent months we'd had little time for each other. Reed was busy at work, while I was preoccupied with Jonathan's injury, physical therapy, and doctor's appointments. My attention was drawn in many directions with every moment spent coordinating activities, homework, and meals for all three boys. I didn't want Michael and Eric to feel neglected, but I didn't stop to think that Reed might feel that way.

One evening in December, Reed watched while I packed school lunches for the next morning. "What are you worrying about?" he asked. "You're not enjoying life. You don't have to sacrifice everything, including yourself."

"What about all the pain he's had to face? He's been through more than we'll ever know. Why did this have to happen to Jonathan?"

"You're living in the past," Reed said. "You need to move ahead. Look at the positive things we have now. We have three wonderful boys, and we have each other."

"Yes," I admitted.

"What about us?" he asked. "When are we going to have time for each other? When are we going to get back on the same track?"

"I couldn't do it without you, Reed."

"That's why we have each other. It's teamwork, remember?"

"I guess I've become paralyzed and fearful of life," I explained. "After what we've been through, I never want to let our boys out of my sight."

"You can't continue to grieve," he said. "That's not helping."

"What should we do?" I asked.

"Remember, we support each other. We're a team. That's what you've always told the boys. We've got to stick together. And you're the glue that holds us together."

"Wow, you make me feel so important."

"And you are. We've never had such a great challenge in our lives. It's a time for us to grow. So please, let's move on with our lives together. Let's enjoy each other and our boys."

"Yes...I'm ready to get back on track. Thanks for reminding me what's important. Now I remember ... you're my strength, always there when I need you...Thanks, Reed."

I needed to reconnect with my own life. But returning to the larger world was difficult for me after so much time focusing on Jonathan and his needs. I hadn't gone to a concert or movie in ages. I'd fallen out of touch with my friends and the events in their lives. I'd forgotten how much I'd always enjoyed our mom's coffee group. After all these months, it was time to get back together with friends.

I called Cecil and arranged to meet her at Starbucks on Friday, our traditional mom's coffee day. She invited Amy and Vicky and Lisa to join us. I was happy to get back to the familiar routine with friends, to laugh and compare notes on raising our kids, to share advice about our lives and the funny things that always seem to happen when you're already late for soccer practice.

Most important was sharing time together. My friends were a source of strength. I don't think they realized how much they meant to me. They helped soothe my tumultuous world and helped me remember who I was. Relationships were everything.

I took long walks with Marissa along the paths in Lucas Valley. She was a sincere friend, a mother of boys, and a good source of advice. Georgia, the mother I'd met in the hospital waiting room, drove across the Bay to get together and keep in touch. Our friendship had grown out of a chance meeting on that night in the hospital filled with so much uncertainty.

Being with friends reminded me how important they were in my life. Reestablishing these relationships gradually helped me feel more confident, and move beyond the shark. I could see brighter days returning.

Over the months, Jonathan and I began to write more seriously. We spent hours together, writing, trying to describe what had happened and how it had changed us. We talked about where our story was headed. Our writing created a dialogue, and I grew to appreciate the depth of his courage and determination. He wanted to hear the story from my point of view, almost like stories I'd told when he was a little boy. Through it all, he seemed resilient; while I was still trying to come to terms with the shark's intrusion into our experience as a family.

I soon realized that writing had become not only a means to record our story, but also a way to understand its impact in our lives. I was searching for lessons in our story and in our lives. For me, writing was an important way to make sense of this overwhelming chapter in our family journey. Gradually we were putting together the pieces, like a series of mosaics. Writing helped me sort out my thoughts and put everything into perspective. It helped me deal with everything we'd faced. Sometimes I could almost hear the sound of the ocean in the words, and often the words and memories brought tears to my eyes.

I began to appreciate that our experience had transformed us. We'd always shared our love of the ocean, but in many ways, that had changed… family togetherness had become an even greater priority than ever. Writing, putting thoughts into words, and letting my anxieties flow like ink onto paper, helped me see that our story continued to unfold in unexpected ways. I began to wonder what the next chapter would be.

In a way, I'd stumbled upon my own best therapy. For months I'd been fighting to stay afloat. Finally I realized that writing was the way to make sense of everything, to gain perspective, to decrease my sense of isolation, to alleviate guilt, and to diminish the images of the shark and the worries I'd been struggling to overcome. There were memories I'd never forget, but stability was gradually returning to my life as I managed to piece together our story. My sense of life expanded and I began to appreciate the simple things, like each new day, the sky, or hearing the voice of a friend. I began to see what was really important to me. But even my own recovery seemed to be a long slow process.

Four months after his release from the hospital, we sent back the well-used CPM Machine. The blue and white truck picked it up. At first, Jonathan's room seemed empty, but he was happy to be free of this encumbrance.

In mid December he faced another surgery. "Your knee is strong and it's time to remove the screw I put in to hold everything together." Dr. Davis said.

I revisited all the anxiety of the previous surgery. I dreaded the drive to the hospital that day, but Jonathan was brave, as always.

The surgery went well, and for him it was only a minor setback. He kept the screw in a jar on his desk. The screw, his scars, and the shark memorabilia were enduring reminders of how fortunate we were.

A week later, I received a phone call from Germany. In perfect English with a German accent, the voice on the phone invited our family to fly to Germany for Jonathan to be honored on a live television program, "People of the Year 1998." This was a special invitation and we didn't want Jonathan to miss it, so Reed and I decided to take all three boys out of school and fly to Cologne, Germany.

Jonathan was honored along with German Chancellor Helmut Kohl and others. He wore an earpiece with a simultaneous interpreter translating the questions and his answers. A life size model of a great white shark hung on stage and the host of the program asked Jonathan to point out the gills that were so important to his survival. His story was broadcast to viewers across Europe.

The next day, we explored the festive outdoor Christmas markets and mingled with happy families in the wintry city of Cologne. The program generated international attention for Jonathan, but most of all, the trip created another memorable family bond for us. It seemed a fitting end to a year that had brought so much unpredictability.

After returning home, we tried to keep television appearances to a minimum, to avoid further disruptions in our lives. When Candace, a producer from the Oprah Show called asking Jonathan to fly to New York the next day, we turned her down. "I can't miss any more school right now," he said. Our friends told us turning down Oprah was a rare and honorable event. Jonathan also turned down Montel Williams, Sara Jessie Raphael, Conan O'Brien and others. We needed to get back to our lives.

For Christmas that year, Jonathan wanted to reconnect with family and friends in the Midwest. We flew to Wisconsin and rented a big house on Lake Geneva. We invited Grandma, aunts, uncles, cousins, and friends for Christmas dinner and, in Midwest tradition, everybody came. Jonathan no longer needed his leg brace, but Grandma noticed he was still limping.

Jonathan practiced running up and down the staircase of the big old house with his cousins, proud that he could do it. On Christmas night we skated on the frozen lake under big yellow floodlights, just like old times when we'd lived in the Midwest, safe and far from sharks.

> *"Life is either a daring adventure or nothing."*
> - Helen Keller

After Christmas break, Jonathan returned to his high school soccer team. He wasn't strong enough to play in the games, so the coach gave him special status as a practice player and made him the team cameraman. He liked the sense of belonging, but even more, he wanted to play.

Jonathan focused on his goals – to be strong, to run, and to swim. He practiced running laps and kicking the ball. These were ambitious goals, but to him, progress seemed slow. Michael and Eric were right there, practicing with him, challenging him to keep trying.

From 1999 – 2002

In January 1999, Dr. John McCosker, the most respected shark expert in the world, invited us for a behind-the-scenes family tour at the Academy of Sciences in San Francisco. As a scientist, he wanted to see Jonathan's scars and hear the details of his face-to-face encounter. We met him at the Academy of Science in Golden Gate Park where he led us down a long flight of stairs, into his basement laboratory lined with shelves and samples from floor to ceiling. Each shelf held jars and bottles with every imaginable kind of fish. He even showed us a large tank that held preserved sharks, many with formidable teeth, but not a single great white shark.

"Great white sharks are rarely ever seen," he explained. "These smaller sharks will give you some perspective." I was a bit hesitant to look at these sharks, and I thought Jonathan might shy away, but he looked at them closely. He studied the teeth and jaws of the different sharks, trying to understand these creatures that were more awesome than he'd ever imagined.

A month later, Jonathan and Dr. McCosker collaborated on a documentary film for the Discovery Channel, with McCosker providing the scientific information and Jonathan giving the perspective of the shark up close. Together they conveyed the message that sharks need our help because humans are more of a danger to sharks than they are to us. In spite of what happened to him, Jonathan wanted to help protect sharks and their environment from pollution, overfishing, shark-finning, and interference from humans. We learned to appreciate the importance of sharks in our world, and despite their power and menacing image, to recognize that they are fragile members of our environment.

"I believe we are all on this earth to
touch other people's lives."
- Jonathan's Dateline NBC interview

In February, 1999 the Producer from Dateline NBC called to schedule the filming of Part II of Jonathan's story. "Are you ready to return to Stinson Beach?" I asked Jonathan, wondering what his response would be.

"Yes, I think it's time for me to see the beach where everything happened," he replied. "But I don't want to go alone."

"Of course we'll go with you, Jonathan. I guess we all have memories to overcome," I said. I thought for a moment about how my fears were so different from his. He was the one who'd lived through it. He would never forget the shark. I would never forget my fear of losing him.

Jonathan was ready to confront his memories. Once again he was pulling me forward too. I couldn't let my fears hold him back. We planned a family day and drove to the beach. When we arrived at the Stinson Beach parking lot, we saw a huge sign with a picture of a great white shark that gave me shivers:

"WARNING – ON AUGUST 26, 1998 A PERSON WAS ATTACKED BY A SHARK HERE AT STINSON BEACH IN 6 FEET OF WATER. BE AWARE OF THE POTENTIAL FOR SHARKS IN SHALLOW WATER, ALONG THE ENTIRE LENGTH OF THE BEACH."

"Well, I guess we know who that person is," Michael said as we paused to read the sign. "But do they really need to warn people that sharks live in the ocean?"

We followed the path up and over the dunes, through the tall, wind-blown beach grass, with Michael and Eric in the lead and Jonathan following close behind. I wondered how this all-too-familiar scene might affect Jonathan but in fact I think it was more difficult for me. We walked through the loose, drifting sand to a high point atop the beach and looked out over the ocean where Jonathan had struggled alone for his life. The beach looked different now, colored by our memories of that day.

Sean, also invited by the Dateline crew, joined us a few minutes later. He and Jonathan stood shoulder to shoulder looking out. I could see that Sean was reliving his memories, just as we were.

Technicians dressed in black jeans and black t-shirts positioned cameras, reflectors, microphones, generators, and gear. They wired Jonathan and Sean for remote sound. Cords crisscrossed the sand from a huge truck that powered the equipment. A man on the beach threw a ball to his dog. Other than that, the beach seemed quiet.

"Hey, Jonathan, it's good to see you. I'll be your sound man for the interview today." The voice belonged to David, our neighbor who'd known Jonathan since grade school. "Dateline hires local people for their crew rather than flying everyone out from New York. So here I am."

"I'm happy to see a familiar face," Jonathan said.

Then we heard another voice. "Good morning, I'm Josh Mankowitz, from NBC news. We're ready to begin the interview," he said. "I'll give a short introduction, and then I'll talk to you and Sean. We'd like a shot of you two walking on the beach together, but we won't ask you to get in the water."

"Well, that's good, because I'm not ready to get back into that water, not today," Jonathan replied.

The camera started rolling and the questions began. Jonathan had become accustomed to speaking in front of a camera and his mind focused on the events of that day. The story he'd told many times, now took on new realism here on the beach where every detail seemed more vivid. This was the beach that had changed our lives. Hearing his words still terrified me.

Finally, Josh paused to look at his notes, thinking about everything Jonathan had said. "Now that you've had a few months to reflect, how do you feel now about the shark that attacked you?" he asked.

"I was swimming in the shark's world," Jonathan said. "The shark belongs there and I was the outsider. In the ocean, there are no boundaries. The shark doesn't know about beaches. The shark is a natural predator, designed to attack. Maybe the shark felt threatened because I was in its environment. Maybe it was trying to defend its territory. The shark thought I was the intruder."

"Are you mad at the shark for what it did to you?" Josh pressed for more.

"What happened to me was not the shark's fault. The shark was doing what it's supposed to do and I ventured into its home. The shark is an important part of the chain that keeps the ocean healthy for all of us to enjoy.

"Should we be afraid of sharks when we swim in the ocean?"

"There are lots of dangers on land too," Jonathan said, "but we don't stay at home because of them. We don't want to live in fear. We can still enjoy the ocean, but we need to remember...sharks live there too."

Josh turned to Sean and asked, "Sean, were you worried about sharks?"

"I had an eerie feeling that day...I'm not sure why. Maybe it was the shadows in the water. Sure, I thought about sharks, like everyone does out there. It's always in the back of your mind, but I never thought it would happen."

"Sean, are you going back into the water?" Josh asked.

"No, I don't think so, at least not anytime soon."

"One last question, Jonathan.... If you do go back out, will you be thinking about sharks?"

"Now, when I think about my experience with the shark, I think about my family. I've learned my family will always be there for me. That's what's important."

Then Josh turned to me. "You're his Mom, what do you think about Jonathan going back into the water?"

"I guess we'll see what Jonathan decides." I smiled at Jonathan and he smiled in return.

"Okay, I'd like a shot of you two on the beach," Josh said.

Jonathan walked tenuously across the uneven sand, revisiting a world he remembered so well. Sean walked slowly at his side. Two surfers sprinted past them to the water while Jonathan walked unsteadily, not at all like the surfer he'd wanted to be.

"Okay, let's get a family scene," said Josh.

We all gathered around Jonathan and ended the story with a game of Frisbee on the beach. We were a family, having fun together again. Even the most frivolous moments had become more meaningful.

"I'm thankful you convinced us to return to Stinson Beach," I said to Josh. "Without a reason, we might not have crossed this hurdle for a long time."

The photographer captured Jonathan's face deep in thought as he looked at the waves, the image of a young man looking out at a world that had changed him forever.

The cameraman packed away his equipment while the crew took down the lights and reflectors. But Josh seemed fascinated by the story and he continued to talk to Jonathan.

"In many ways, you seem to have turned your shark attack into something positive," he said. "You're an amazing young man. It's not that I envy what you've had to go through, but your experience seems to have made you a richer person."

Jonathan paused, and thought about his comment. "My family's helped me through it, and I think we've learned a lot. We're a good team and we appreciate each other."

I looked at the crashing waves and realized how far we'd come. Our experience had enriched our lives. Jonathan's survival was truly a great gift. In his eyes I could see his dream of getting back to the waves. My dream was for him to be well and strong enough to try.

> *"Go Confidently in the direction of your dreams.*
> *Live the life you've imagined."*
>
> - Thoreau

When Dateline "Survivor" aired on national television in March of 1999, Stone Phillips introduced Jonathan's story with dramatic music and underwater footage of a great white shark. I didn't want to imagine what it was really like. Our friends and family across the country were watching. At home, we re-lived the day of the shark with Jonathan and I thought of all the miracles we were blessed to receive.

We'd all grown closer over the months. I could see how important we were to each other, individually and together as a family. Jonathan had grown stronger in every way. Michael and Eric were given an opportunity to see the world through the eyes of experience. I'd balanced my own life with family and friends again. Reed was our foundation. We were a family profoundly changed. The experience had deepened and widened our sense of life. Our dreams were still alive. Together we could get through anything.

The days and months that followed turned out to be days of great happiness, days to remember, when we lived up to ourselves and our promises to each other. Jonathan's strength and spirit exceeded my dreams as well as the doctor's cautious predictions made that summer night in August, so many months earlier.

One day we received a letter from Gordon Radley, a neighbor we'd never met, and President of Lucasfilm at Skywalker Ranch in Lucas Valley not far from us. "I was reading recently how your son is doing," he wrote. "I continue to marvel at his fortitude, courage and bravery...I would say he is lucky and you are fortunate, but that would not give him the credit he is due." Jonathan accepted Gordon's invitation to join him for lunch at Skywalker Ranch. We were happy to receive so much encouragement from others who cared.

Working to realize his vision, Jonathan returned to the St. Ignatius high school swimming pool. Starting out slowly, he swam laps, working to improve his strength. "High School Sports Focus," a Bay Area sports program, came to school to film his return to the pool. To him, this was no big deal, the swimming or the television cameras. Getting back to the water was just part of what he needed to do to get strong and overcome obstacles.

With training and exercise his limp became less noticeable. He continued to work hard, making steady progress until he could ride a bike and run.

"I love to accomplish things that people didn't expect me to achieve," he said, reminding us the doctors had cautioned that his recovery might be limited. Jonathan showed us that if we believed in ourselves, we could go beyond everyone's expectations, even our own.

"You've achieved your goal - to become an athlete again. I'm proud of you," I said.

"One more big goal yet to be reached," he reminded me. I knew he meant surfing.

By the summer of 1999, life at home had returned to normal, whatever that might be. The shark was mentioned less frequently, but never to be forgotten by any of us or by our friends.

I began to feel a resurgence of energy and enthusiasm for living. I began to make sense of my world and tried to savor each moment, not to live in fear. I'd come to realize that I could not let myself regret the day of the shark, because we'd learned so much. That single day had brought us to a better understanding of ourselves and closer to each other.

Throughout it all, Reed and I had grown closer too. The rocky period following Jonathan's injury, when everything seemed like it might fall apart, had taught me to value Reed's support and love in new ways. Now I truly appreciated the relationships in my life. My beliefs about the beauty of the ocean, the importance of its creatures, and the value of friendships were reinforced by our experience. All those days and months of uncertainty had become memories to cherish, not to be feared.

The secret for me was finding balance between my dreams and what actually came into my life. I'd always loved the ocean. What came into my life was the shark. I was beginning to realize that in some ways, the shark was a blessing I'd failed to appreciate.

I was becoming aware of how stories create meaning in our lives, help us remember our path, and help us find direction. I needed to continue writing, to record our story. I was grateful for the lessons we'd learned from the shark. How could I fail to appreciate an experience that taught me so much? Whenever Jonathan told his story, I realized he was the hero, leading the way for each one of us. He was confident, accepting of the world, and I should be too.

I was beginning to see that Jonathan's survival was not an ending, but the beginning of a longer journey. His was a story that had transformed our lives. I'd learned about my faith, my family, and the challenges we all face in our lives, especially as parents. Worry for the well-being of our children never ceases. And wanting the approval and reassurance of our parents is eternal, for we are all children.

My mother was at the heart of my experience. She was my biggest supporter. I still called her often for advice, or just to hear her cheerful voice. Her constant support and the values I'd learned were timeless. I'd always look to her for guidance.

Reed worked late almost every night. "I'm the absentee dad, always at work," he joked, but I knew better. He'd drop everything in a moment if I needed him. His laughter kept me on track, reminding me to appreciate the days I spent at home with our boys, and not to live in the past or worry about the future. He was strong and devoted to our family without showing it.

Relationships became treasures in my life. I became more open and more involved with my friends. I realized how much we all needed each other and I wanted to be there for others, as they were for me. I wanted to hear their stories too. Old connections felt even more important.

The shark had led us to an awareness of the thin line between life and death. This awareness didn't make me a different person on the outside, but helped me reassess my values, find my path, and remember who I was. It helped me see the gifts in my life. I learned to appreciate everything more than before. I discovered how important we are to each other. Ours was a story with many positive lessons and answers to our prayers... Jonathan's survival and a stronger family. But our story hadn't ended. I was waiting for new chapters to unfold.

> *"Sharks don't mean to eat people...*
> *Maybe the shark thought I was trying to hurt it...*
> *Maybe it was afraid of me...*
> *Maybe it was all just a big mistake."*
> **- Jonathan, at Mary Silviera Grade School**

In May 2000, Jonathan graduated from St. Ignatius High School and was accepted to the University of California at Berkeley as a freshman. We were excited and proud, but on move-in day in early September, I noticed he seemed reluctant to leave home. He lingered in our familiar surroundings, playing the drums in the garage and reminiscing over childhood memories. He'd learned to live in the moment, enjoying life at a more relaxed pace, even on an ordinary day. I wondered if his experience had made leaving home more difficult.

He moved into his dorm on Telegraph Avenue near campus, but never stayed away from home and family for long. He came home most weekends to be with his brothers. Once again, I could see the strength of family in our lives. Home was a place to be together and safe.

At Cal, he was invited to lecture on the subject of sharks for Cal Oceanography classes. Students listened with typical detachment and emotionless faces as he began to convey statistics, telling the students how rarely sharks attack people. "Then, when I told them I was one of those statistics, their eyes widened and everyone woke up." His lectures were well received and the students asked him countless questions about sharks and his experience. Jonathan took the opportunity to convey the need to protect sharks, describing how fragile they are despite their frightening image, and explaining that sharks are more threatened by humans than we are by them.

The San Francisco Giants invited Jonathan to throw out the first pitch at a baseball game. As he stepped out onto the huge field at Candlestick Park, the billboard and the announcer introduced him as, "Shark Man" and "a survivor." The crowd cheered for him as he smiled and took the spotlight.

Later that year, Jonathan joined Peter Benchley, the author of *Jaws* and *Shark Trouble,* for "Shark Day" at the Academy of Sciences in Golden Gate Park. The event was sponsored by WildAid to create awareness and to help protect sharks from overfishing and shark-finning, the practice of killing sharks just for their fins. Jonathan answered questions and handed out information about sharks. Benchley tried to soften the unfortunate image of the man-eater he'd created in *Jaws.* He joked with Jonathan, "I've written a lot about sharks, but you've survived an encounter I've never experienced, up close and personal with a shark."

One weekend we drove south along the Pacific Coast to the Monterey Bay Aquarium. Jonathan wanted to see the white shark that was accidentally caught in a fisherman's net and placed on display in a large tank with other fish at the aquarium. It was a rare opportunity to see one of the few white sharks ever held in captivity. I admired Jonathan for wanting to see it, and I realized that gradually sharks were becoming a more acceptable part of our lives.

The young shark was only 4 ½ feet long, but it drew a big crowd. Its presence increased awareness of a predator about which much is known, but much remains to be learned. The great white shark is a creature hardly ever seen. Jonathan wanted to see this smaller version of his attacker.

"That great white shark looks like a Ferrari in a tank full of Volkswagens," he said as he watched it swimming with the other fish. "Its movements are so sleek and effortless. Without even trying, it seems to dominate the others." Later we learned the little shark had to be released because it started taking bites out of its tank-mates. This little white shark was an apex predator, even in captivity.

Later that year, Jonathan was interviewed by the National Geographic Channel for a documentary about the Red Triangle called, "Shark Battleground – The Red Triangle." The filming lasted all day with cameras and crews at Cronkhite Beach. The following week, the film crew invited Jonathan, Reed, and me to join them for an all day boat trip to the Farallone Islands with a naturalist and the crew, hoping to film live footage of great white sharks. These islands form the tip of the Red Triangle, part of the national marine sanctuary off the coast of San Francisco, and are home to seals, sea lions, birds, and great white sharks. We were warned that we might see a shark attack, especially with so many seals in the water offering a plentiful food supply. I had to admit I was fearful of seeing a great white shark in the wild, especially attacking a seal, but Jonathan was brave and ready to observe nature. We didn't see a shark after all, but the humpback whales put on a spectacular show, breaching and slapping the water with their huge fins.

The next summer, while I was training for a marathon, I went running with Jonathan in the Lucas Valley hills. I was amazed at how far he'd come in his healing, remembering how the doctors had said he might never run again. "You're a gazelle," I shouted to him as he sprinted joyfully past me up the next hill. His long legs stretched out gracefully and he was light on his feet as he flew past me along the path into the wind. His life was breezing along, past mine, and I no longer needed to worry. Another miracle, I thought, thankful for his ongoing recovery and his enthusiasm for everything. Over the years, he'd healed from the inside, learning from his experiences how to strengthen his body and renew his spirit. He was strong and whole and eager for life.

Michael and Eric, now in high school, started going to the beach on weekends with their friends, toting boogie boards and skim boards. Soon they were learning to surf, braving cold water, harsh waves, and other perils of Northern California. But days at the beach were never as much fun without Jonathan, and they wanted their brother to join them.

Jonathan's friend, Charlie, an avid surfer, pestered him endlessly to get back into the water. "Jon, you've got a greater chance of getting hit on the head by a coconut than getting attacked by another shark. What are you waiting for? Grab a board and come out with us."

Despite the fear he remembered so well, Jonathan wanted to rediscover the joys of the ocean. The memories and the fear held him back. It was only a matter of time before he would be confident enough to move ahead with his plans to get back to the water. For a time I'd existed in a kind of limbo, loving the ocean but afraid of it. And yet I knew that as a family, as much as we'd tried to forget the ocean, we couldn't ignore its pull in our lives.

Jonathan started going to the beach with Michael and Eric, but he'd stay on shore, watching while they surfed. They bought him a skim board so he could have fun at the beach without getting into the water. He learned to ride the ribbon of water at the edge of the sand on his skim board. Sometimes he'd get wet, yet he stayed in the shallow water where he could still feel safe.

Jonathan watched surf videos and read books about surfing and the ocean. He was inspired by the dramatic stories of crashing waves and surfing adventures. At the beach and he watched the surfers and observed different surfing styles and types of boards. He studied, read, and learned the art of surfboard shaping. He spent hours making a surfboard and designing his own logo for it. Then he proudly gave it to Reed as a surprise birthday gift. Using his skills and working with his hands to create the surfboard gave him a new perspective on the art of surfing. Jonathan was searching for his own ways to reconnect with the ocean.

For a long time, the surfboard he'd made stood in the corner of our living room, almost like a work of art. We admired its smooth lines and the colorful logo, "Jonnyboy Surfboards." No one suggested we take it out and try it in the ocean, and yet I knew that day was coming. He dreamed of getting back in the water, not just to prove to himself he could do it, but because the ocean was his love.

Jonathan knew I was fearful, unwilling to forget our close call. "Jonathan, I don't want to lose you."

"Mom, it's something I need to do. Fear might always be with me in the ocean," he said, "But I refuse to let fear stop me. I still remember all the reasons why I love the ocean."

Not knowing what else to do, I called my mother later that day. "Mother, I'm faced with some tough decisions here. Jonathan wants to go back to the ocean. What should I say?"

"We can't plan every step in life. Remember, Margie-dear, just take one day at a time."

"But I don't know what to say," I pleaded.

"Just let him make his choices. Your support will give him confidence in himself." Her encouragement reassured me. She was always the eternal optimist and I wanted to be as resilient as she was. She reminded me we could not say no to life. After we hung up, I prayed for guidance, and I knew she was praying too.

The shark was a part of our family story that was shaping our future too. Jonathan and I continued writing, trying to piece together its impact

in our lives and trying to see the experience through each other's eyes. The
story was interwoven throughout our lives.

One afternoon, Jonathan and I talked about where our story was heading. "What will the ending be?" I asked.

"The next chapter should be my return to the ocean," he said. I knew
he wasn't joking.

Jonathan and Grandma at home together, filled with positive energy

Returning to John Muir Hospital for doctor's appointments

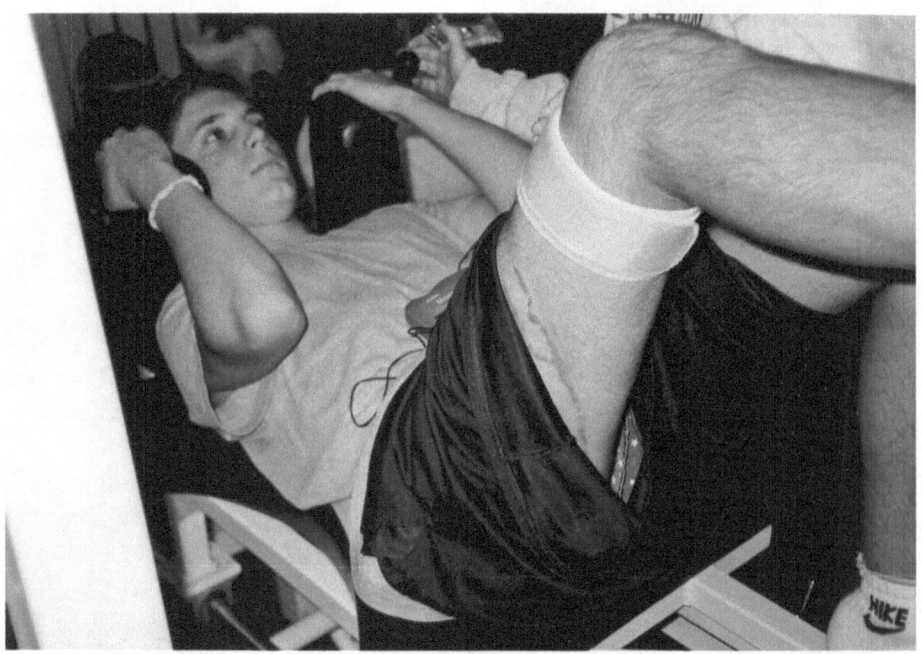

Jonathan working on rehab

Our family celebration – a backyard Victory Party for Jonathan

Filming for Dateline NBC at Stinson Beach

The Dateline NBC crew at Stinson Beach

Eric, Michael, and Jonathan at Stinson for the filming of Dateline NBC

**Jonathan "AKA Shark Man" throwing out the first pitch,
Giants vs. Padres, at Candlestick Park**

Jonathan appearing on *Fox Mornings on 2* **with host, Ross McGowan**

Jonathan and Peter Benchley, author of *Jaws* **and** *Shark Trouble*

Jonathan at the WildAid information table on Shark Day:
"How Much Do You Know About Sharks?"

Jonathan wearing his shark swim cap.
Getting back to swimming at Championships.

Jonathan made a surfboard with his own logo, *Jonnyboy Surfboards*

On the boat at the Farallone Islands, the tip of the Red Triangle

"I must go down to the seas again,
for the call of the running tide
Is a wild call and a clear call that may not be denied;
All I ask is a windy day with the white clouds flying,
And the flung spray and the blown spume,
and the sea-gulls crying."
                                        - "Sea Fever," by John Masefield

March 2002

Four years had passed, and Jonathan was beginning to feel more comfortable with the ocean again. He accompanied his brothers and friends to the beach, but he mostly stayed on shore to watch. One day after returning home, he told me candidly, "I thought I might get into the water, but once I got there, I was too afraid to try."

His enthusiasm told me we were ready to begin a new chapter. The attack by the shark had taught him to treasure life - I could see it in his eyes and hear it in his words. "I'm determined not to let one encounter with a shark stop me from enjoying the ocean," he said. Jonathan was reminding me that a new season was beginning. We needed to pursue new beginnings, and Jonathan was leading the way. I hoped I was ready for whatever might come.

"Mom, I'm ready to get back into the ocean," Jonathan announced one afternoon in March 2002. "I checked the surf report and it looks like a good swell coming in. How about a family trip to the beach this weekend? I'd like to try surfing again."

I hesitated, not knowing what to say, trying to collect my thoughts. I'd known this day was coming, but I wasn't prepared for it. I wanted him to feel confident, and yet I worried about the outcome. Already I was worrying about his safety, wondering what emotions it might trigger again – for him and for me. I didn't want him in that water ever again. It was an emotional conversation.

"Jonathan, I know how important this is to you, but...."

"Mom, I still love the ocean. Ever since I was a little boy, you've taught me to appreciate the water. The ocean is where I find solitude, relaxation, and time to reflect. Surfing takes me away from the hectic pace of life and all the little details. Life always looks different when I'm out there in the water, away from shore. The ocean gives me a different perspective. And it's always beautiful."

"I understand. But do you think you can ever go back into the water, after everything that's happened?"

"I know it'll be difficult, Mom...for both of us. I admit I'm still not comfortable in the open water, but I don't want that fear to stay with me forever," he said.

"No one would blame you if you never set foot in the ocean again."

"I know, but getting back in the water is something I have to do," he reminded me. "And something I want to do. For myself."

"I don't want to take a chance of losing you, Jonnyboy."

"Don't worry, Mom. This is something to celebrate. Achieving another goal."

Late that night I reflected on our conversation and talked it over with Reed. I was struggling with how to handle the uncertainty that was entering our lives again.

"I'm worried....He wants to go back to the ocean. What do you think we should do?" I asked.

"I think you should let him decide," Reed said. "He needs the freedom to dream his own dreams. And we'll support him all the way."

"I don't know why it's taking so long for me to recover from the memories of the shark...I guess it's my fear of losing him to the ocean."

"Yes, but for Jonathan, surfing might offer the key to overcoming his own fears and finding satisfaction. You have to let him go." I knew Reed was right. And I remembered Jonathan's frequent advice to others, *always keep trying*. He was not about to give up now.

"I guess we've all come a long way in our journey," I replied.

"Let's keep moving forward," Reed said, "Besides, I'll even let him try out my new surfboard, the one that's standing in the living room collecting dust." He smiled and gave me a hug.

Jonathan was reaching another milestone. It was such a rewarding experience to share each step of his recovery and his journey with him; I was proud to be his mother and a part of his life. Now we were taking another step, and with each step Jonathan was teaching us to live our best lives every day. Watching him progress, I'd learned to celebrate life. The difficult times had helped me understand how infinitely rich life is in every way and that so many of the things I'd worried about before had no importance. Now, I had to pick up the threads I had dropped. This was a time to rejoice. It was a family journey too.

We decided the following Saturday would be our beach day. But more than that, it would be the long-awaited surfing day. Reed and I would be there to share this milestone with our boys. I was beginning to overcome my initial hesitation, and I wanted to support Jonathan and cheer for him.

Without realizing it, I'd started to see the positive side of the shark experience. Still, I'd always have worries.

We all piled into the Toyota minivan and headed for Cronkhite Beach. Jonathan had chosen this small protected beach just north of the Golden Gate Bridge where the waves break close to shore in a sheltered cove. We all wanted to avoid going back to Stinson, where too many memories lurked. From the freeway, we took the Sausalito Exit and followed the road up and over the Marin Headlands. From the top, the spreading view of San Francisco Bay, the Golden Gate Bridge, and the Pacific Ocean reminded me of the morning I'd stopped there alone, on the day of the shark attack. But today we were together and ready for anything, I hoped.

We followed the sweeping road out to the coast, past chaparral, manzanita, and mountain lilac. We noticed a family of California quail parading along the side of the road with their feathery topknots. Bunnies scattered into the grass. The fog thickened as we neared the ocean, something we'd now come to expect after living in California for almost fifteen years.

"The surf looks good today…it's not too windy, and the waves are holding up," Michael said as Cronkhite Beach and the lagoon came into view. "It's a perfect day."

From the distance, the surface of the ocean appeared smooth, interrupted only by the waves crashing onto the pebbly beach. The fog was lifting, and the day was clear with an offshore breeze and waves breaking in perfect sets close to shore. The waves were rolling fast and the wind gave an air of excitement to the day. We could see a handful of surfers in the water, their black wetsuits shining like the wet fur of harbor seals. I wondered if Jonathan's heart was pounding as much as mine.

In the parking lot, the three brothers tugged their wetsuits over their long legs and arms while Reed helped them unload their boards. I rolled up my jeans and walked across the wet sand to feel the chill of the water against my feet. I stood alone at the edge of the world. I hadn't been at the beach for ages, and I was almost surprised to find it hadn't changed. But everything looked brighter than I remembered. A mist hit my lips and the salty air held the promise of new beginnings. From where I stood, the waves appeared higher than the land and the thin line of the distant horizon stretched forever.

I saw challenges ahead but more than that, I remembered those we'd overcome. Now, for the first time since Jonathan's attack, I looked at the ocean in a new way. I simply saw its majesty, and it was breathtaking.

I remembered Jonathan's words, "Mom, the ocean is always beautiful." He'd said it many times. Now I believed him. The ocean was always beautiful. Always waiting for us.

With no conversation and little hesitation, Jonathan now 19, Michael 17, and Eric 14, crossed the beach with their surfboards under their arms. Jonathan had grown strong and his limp was hardly noticeable. His wounds had healed but his scars would always be a sign of what he'd survived. His resilient spirit was stronger than ever.

Eager but tentative they crossed the pebbly sand. I watched every step. No one looked back. They hovered at the shore together. They were a team, ready to try surfing again.

"The waves are picking up. I think I'm ready," Jonathan said to his brothers.

"Don't worry, we'll be right beside you," Michael said.

"Let's go...It's the day we've been waiting for," said Eric.

Jonathan looked to me for approval. "I'm watching," I replied.

Reed and I looked out at the ocean and at our boys, observing the story of our lives. I could hear the call of a foghorn somewhere along the coast near San Francisco. Surfers rode the waves and the wind took our breath away. Once again I felt the pull of the ocean in our lives.

Michael and Eric ventured into the water first, standing ankle-deep, waiting for Jonathan. He stood at the edge, studying the surface of the ocean. No one said anything. The conditions were nearly ideal, with shoulder high waves breaking into smooth arcs coming in long sweeps, fast and clean. The sky had cleared, and the water sparkled with reflections of deep cobalt blue. The ocean beckoned.

Jonathan stepped cautiously into the water, one hand on his board floating alongside him. He focused on finding the best spot to paddle out. He walked slowly but resolutely, moving watchfully into deeper water, letting the waves wash against him. The dark water was full of shadows. He paused waist-deep to look ahead. He was almost there.

Michael and Eric stretched out on their boards but didn't paddle out, they waited for Jonathan. Finally, Michael shouted, "C'mon, grab your board and hop on. What are you waiting for?"

"Okay, let's go after this wave."

Jonathan tossed his surfboard across the water and launched himself over the next wave. I imagined the rush of cold water flooding his wetsuit.

I heard Michael's voice over the sound of the waves, "Hey, Jonathan. Let's get past that break, out to where it's calm."

"Okay, I'm with you," Jonathan said. "Let's stay together...."

They plunged forward into the surf, paddling hard, pulling through the water, shoulder-to-shoulder. A crashing wave tossed their boards but they held on. Jonathan paddled out into the freedom of the ocean he loved so much. Michael and Eric were right beside him.

Reed and I watched from shore as they moved out into the surf. Together the three brothers created a striking silhouette. They pushed their boards down, diving under each new wave as it broke. They paddled harder, moving away from shore into the deep cold water. Jonathan paddled closer to Michael.

Finally they reached the calm water, past the breaking waves where they could rest and float. They joined a few other surfers who were clustered together, waiting for the waves to pick up, floating low in the water, legs dangling off their boards, riding the swells.

Eric started splashing his brothers. Michael responded with more splashing and soon all three were engaged in a water skirmish that turned a serious moment into fun. I could see their love for each other and the strong bond they shared.

Then all of a sudden, in the midst of the fun, Jonathan yelled, to his brothers, "Hey… Watch out. There's something in the water."

Instantly, he panicked. I could see the memories flooding back. I could feel the fear in his voice.

"Something brushed my leg…"

He jerked his board around sharply and started heading in, paddling hard. Michael and Eric quickly moved closer to him, staying with him, paddling toward shore. By now they were back in shallow water again. Then I heard the explosion of the next wave as it crashed.

At the shore, Jonathan jumped off his board, bolted to his feet, and rushed toward the beach. I was as alarmed as he was. He turned to look back, then he heard Michael's voice calling to him.

"Wait...Jonathan. Relax," Michael said. "I think it's only seaweed."

Michael dove down and quickly surfaced, holding a long piece of kelp. The thick strand of ropey seaweed had been floating just under the surface of the water.

I took a deep breath, trying to comprehend Jonathan's fear. Then I saw the relief on the faces of my boys. Jonathan looked shaken, but now reassured.

"That was silly...I guess I over-reacted," he said almost sheepishly. He was now standing on shore, trying to make light of his panic. But we all understood.

"It's okay...nothing to worry about. Let's paddle back out," Eric said.

"Wait a few minutes...I'm not sure I'm ready." I knew Jonathan was fighting to overcome the memory of the shark, torn between fear and his love of the ocean. But he knew what he wanted to do. I knew it wasn't easy, but he was determined.

"Okay, I think I can do it now," Jonathan said. He turned to the ocean once again and started to paddle, floating outstretched on top of his board. Reed smiled at me as we noticed Jonathan pulling through the water in a steady rhythm, chest pressed against his board, but holding his feet high, not letting them dangle into the water. He was easy to spot from shore.

Jonathan moved out into deeper water. Michael and Eric were right there with him. The three brothers paddled together, with long strokes and strong arms.

When they reached a spot beyond the breaking waves where the water was calm, they sat on their boards and floated over the swells for a long time, looking out across the shadowy surface of the ocean.

A beautiful wave began to break, shouldering into a perfect curl. The surfers quickly lined up, ready to catch the wave. Jonathan turned his board and paddled hard with the oncoming swell. His board dropped down the face of the wave as it broke, gaining speed, until he popped to his feet. The rush of the water lifted his board and carried him across the face of the breaking wave. Sunlight touched the crest of the wave and from the shore I could see the smile on his face. In that ray of light, I could see my hopes for our future. He was on top of the world. He basked in the glow of triumph, riding the wave in an ocean wider than the sky.

His board raced across the wave with the water propelling him faster. He was at home in the ocean where so much had happened. Michael and Eric shouted with joy, happy to be in the water with their brother again.

Reed and I found a bench high on the beach with a view of the ocean and sat there shoulder to shoulder for a long time, reflecting on the day. We watched as they laughed and paddled and surfed together until the sun was low.

After all these months and years, we'd come back to the ocean. There at the coast, over that long afternoon, surrounded by my family, I observed the beauty of the ocean like I'd never seen it before. Now I simply looked at the ocean and admired its magnificence.

I could see our emerging connection with the ocean, one that was undeniable, yet hard to explain. I felt the rush of understanding and new energy in our lives. The ocean had become a part of our family history and a part of our lives. I recalled the lessons I'd learned and the joys I'd found since the day of the shark. At least for now, my fears and memories of the shark faded into the distant horizon. Until now, I'd failed to grasp the true meaning of the ocean and its importance in our lives. We'd crossed that thin line back to safety. As a family, we'd learned to appreciate each other. And we'd learned to love the ocean despite the shark attack, perhaps even more because of it.

As I watched the sky turn from orange-red to bluish-purple I thought about how extraordinary life was and how I'd learned to cherish each day. With the great Pacific before me, and my boys surfing together, I was sure it couldn't get any better than this. I was grateful to share this moment with my family.

"It's been quite a day," Reed said.

"Yes, a beautiful day."

Jonathan back on his board in the ocean, with Michael and Eric

3 Brothers, paddling out together

Afterward

"The sea is a continual miracle...
The fishes that swim - the motion of the waves...
What stranger miracles are there?"
                                        - Walt Whitman

In the summer of 2005, we all went to Hawaii for a family vacation. Something drew us back to the ocean again and again. I'd decided that learning to surf was the next step for me in our unfolding story. I wanted to share the challenge of surfing and experience the ocean in a new way. Surfing with my family would be the ultimate adventure in our journey back to the ocean. The warm water of Honolulu was the perfect spot.

Reed, Jonathan, Michael, Eric and I rented colorful boards right on the beach and headed into the water. Michael and Eric had given me some pointers on how to pop up to my feet and how to stand on the board, demonstrating on the floor of our hotel room the night before. I'd watched them surf many times...this shouldn't be too difficult, I thought.

Paddling out through oncoming waves was the most challenging thing I'd ever done. Getting out past the breaking waves was much more difficult than I expected. My arms burned and my neck ached. The waves battered me and I had to fight to get through each one. I was apprehensive as I moved farther from the safety of the shore. Each wave pushed me back, threatening to overwhelm me and toss me off my board.

Engulfed in the foam of the crashing surf, I felt the real power of the ocean. It was touch and go for me, I kept paddling, with hardly enough strength to overcome each new wave and recover before the next one hit.

I wondered if I had the stamina for surfing, but I could hear Jonathan behind me shouting, commanding, "Don't give up, mom... Paddle hard into this wave... hold onto your board....head straight into it...good, keep going." He encouraged me and praised me, teaching me technique and determination. "Just remember," he said, "the ocean keeps going, and never stops." I knew he meant I had to keep going too.

"Okay, get some speed, to get through this next wave," he urged. I kept going until my strength was gone and my muscles were trembling. Jonathan was right there and he kept me going. Finally, when the biggest wave of all was about to hit me, he reached forward and gave my board a push to give me some momentum. It worked. I moved ahead with one last surge. I made it past the waves. I was finally out there.

He'd reminded me the struggle is not over when you get tired. *"Never give up."* He'd said it many times. I thought of him facing the shark, not stopping and never giving up. He'd shown us all how to fight through things to reach that feeling of accomplishment.

Beyond the breaking waves, I stretched out on my long board, floating over the swells in the warm clear water and took a deep breath. As I watched the other surfers and admired my new perspective, viewing the land from the water, I realized how refreshing it was. Jonathan was right; life does look different out there away from everything.

The swells rocked my board. The sound of waves crashing around me was louder than I'd ever expected. Sounds of the water drowned out everything else. The horizon rose and fell. The sky above me glimmered. My fears diminished for the moment. The sun felt warm again my back and I was one with the beauty of the ocean and wide sky. Jonathan, Michael, Eric, and Reed surrounded me, happy to have me share their favorite pastime.

A few surfers floated not far away. I stayed to one side, at the end of the line, observing, trying to learn from the others, and watching the waves breaking on the reef. I was joyful to be part of the scene. The wild ocean was a new world for me and I was happy to enter.

"Here comes a good wave," Jonathan shouted. I watched it rise above me, I saw the other surfers scramble, and I saw whitewater breaking down the line. Surfers started to paddle, heading into the crest of the wave. Now it was my turn. As the wave approached, I clenched the sides of my surfboard then started paddling until suddenly I felt the water pull me forward at a terrifying speed. My board tipped from side to side and flipped me upside down into the surf. I surfaced quickly, with saltwater stinging my nose, grabbed my board and climbed back on. I struggled to paddle back out through the waves again. By now I was totally exhausted.

"Let's try again," I said, catching my breath.

"Okay, get ready," Jonathan said. "And no more wimpy paddling. Get those arms deep, dig in and pull the water."

"Okay, I'll try." Jonathan lined up my board, pointing me straight toward shore. My anxiety intensified, not knowing what to expect if I caught a wave. But I didn't want to give up and miss this fantastic moment.

"Now...Start paddling." I felt him launch my board forward, pushing me into the rising wave. "Harder, paddle...paddle... don't stop...keep paddling...now pop up...." I was on my own.

I heard his voice behind me, urging, instructing me what to do. I pulled with both arms together. And then suddenly I felt the powerful rush of the wave. I was nervous but excited. I pushed myself up and tried to get my feet under me. My stomach was filled with butterflies. My board wobbled unsteadily. I tried to adjust my feet to keep from falling. Then, all of a sudden, I realized I was standing and the wave was pushing me forward. Suddenly my fear turned to joy. "I did it," I shouted to myself out loud. "I caught a wave."

Then I heard Reed, Michael, and Eric cheering too. "Hooray...You did it, Mom."

Now I understood the challenge and the thrill of catching a wave. Then I looked beside me, surprised to see Jonathan right there, standing on his board looking confident, riding the wave. Michael, Eric and Reed caught the wave too. We were surfing together and I loved it.

Jonathan was right after all – if you think you can do it, and you don't give up, you can do it. Everything came together at that moment...I was one with the waves and the ocean...And we were together as a family. Nothing could compare to this.

Epilogue

"It is not society that is to guide and save the creative hero,
but precisely the reverse....the influence
of a vital person vitalizes"

\- Joseph Campbell

In 2005, the year after his graduation from Cal, Jonathan made good on his promise to try to make a difference in the world. "I want to share the lessons I've learned to help others face the challenges in their lives," he said, not yet realizing that with these words the direction of his life had already detoured down a new path. Once again, it seemed we had the shark to thank.

He founded Future Leaders For Peace, a non-profit organization dedicated to helping children improve their relationships and their lives. With advice and help from his mentors, Richard Hunter and Michael Pritchard, he learned how to run a business and how to inspire young people. He began speaking to groups of school children, determined to help them in their struggles, just as so many had helped him. His shark story was the perfect lead-in to capture the attention of his listeners.

"When the shark attacked me, I learned that life is fragile," Jonathan said to a group of sixth graders at Miller Creek, his own middle school. "I suddenly realized how quickly it could all be taken from me...my life, my family, and my friends. Now I appreciate everything more."

Soon Jonathan began taking his message to thousands of young people at assemblies across the Bay Area, and as far away as Hawaii, and South Africa. He met with foundations and funders who could help. Demand for his programs increased. Before long, Jonathan was on his way to a thriving business with a purpose – to help others face challenges in their lives.

Jonathan continues to search for new opportunities to give back the blessings he's received, inspiring and helping young people. He shares a simple message – the importance of our relationships with others. "If everything had been taken from me that day, and I had only an hour to live, I'd be thinking about how important my friends and family are to me."

He reminds his young listeners how quickly everything could be taken away – something he realized on the day of the shark. His assemblies and *"Be the Change"* workshops increase awareness, helping young people to improve their lives through communication, honesty, listening, leadership and goal setting. Reinforcing these values he hopes to create a ripple effect that will spread to others into the future.

Working with young people, Jonathan has found new direction and meaning in his own life. Helping others, he's helped himself. Teaching others to find their way has helped him find his way too. The lessons he learned from the shark inspired him to share what he'd learned with others. And, he's found a meaningful path to follow.

In 2006, he published a children's book, *Don't Fear the Shark*, a simple metaphor for our lives, with illustrations by his childhood friend and artist, Robby Singler. Jonathan tells a story of hope that reminds us not to hate our attacker, but to value our relationships with each other and the earth's creatures.

Jonathan uses the story of his shark attack to encourage others to respect sharks and the environment. He's become a motivational speaker with a message about life and the importance of relationships, in nature and with each other. Surviving the shark attack has directed his path in unexpected ways, and he has a lifetime of experience yet to come.

In June, 2008, Jonathan received the Jefferson Award for public service, recognizing his work in the community. The same determination he'd used to fight off the great white has helped him to share what he's learned with children and adults.

In September 2009, Jonathan pushed his courage one step further and achieved a goal – to swim the Tiburon Mile. This annual race from Angel

Island to Tiburon takes place in the cold open water of the bay, easily 200 feet deep. When Michael swam the race in 2002, Jonathan was afraid to try. Tiburon means "shark" in Spanish.

As Jonathan stepped out of the water at the finish line I could see his broad smile and his exuberance. "I decided to do it, even though I'll admit I had moments of worry. I needed to be in a group so I could get back out there and enjoy swimming in the bay, and to prove to myself I could do it."

In many ways, the shark was the continuation of an ongoing relationship with the ocean for Jonathan and for our family. Jonathan's love of the ocean, and ours, has become stronger since that memorable day. In 2009, after a surf trip to El Salvador with his brothers, Jonathan said, "El Salvador means the Savior…The waves were our savior." Without realizing it, over time I've come to see the positive side of the shark experience as it continues to evolve.

One day not long ago, Jonathan revealed in an interview, "I'm more fascinated now than ever by the ocean…I find myself going back more often, to learn, understand, and relax. Ironically, my experience with the shark strengthened my ties to the ocean. I still surf with my brothers, Michael and Eric, and with my friends. I want to experience the world…and I won't let fear stop me from living. I survived one big test in life, but no doubt there will be more."

Throughout his childhood, I'd never realized that Jonathan's spirit of adventure was so compelling. How could I have missed it…even as a little boy his exploits climbing trees, exploring cornfields, and swimming out into deep water all had something in common. Even now, the shark has not extinguished his spirit. In a recent interview for a new documentary called *Predators,* Jonathan confirmed, "The moment you step into the water, it's completely wild… that's what I love about it… I love that thin line between what's safe and what's not safe."

"Eternity isn't some later time...
The experience of Eternity right here
and now is the function of life...
if you don't get it here you won't get it anywhere."
- Joseph Campbell

Having experienced the shark attack, or maybe because of it, we are forever changed. As a family, we are stronger and more resilient. In many ways, we have learned the redeeming power of the ocean. We are connected to the ocean and to others who love it. We find peace, solitude, and inspiration at the ocean where cares fade into the beauty of nature. We have a greater awareness of our own lives, the creatures of the ocean, and the world around us. We know that we enter the ocean, and the greater world, on nature's terms, subject to change without notice.

As a mother, I cherish our joyful moments, and yet I will never forget the dangers and the challenges we've faced. I realize now more than ever how important we are to each other. I know how life can change in a moment. Whenever we come or go, we hug each other, remembering and appreciating each day together.

Most of all, Jonathan has inspired me. My son has become my hero in countless ways. He's accepted his path with courage and humor, meeting every obstacle head-on. And yet he's done so much more than just survive. Jonathan has led us to new ways of seeing the wonder in our lives and in the ocean. He's taught us the joys of family and friendship. As a result of the shark, our lives are forever enriched.

I don't know where Jonathan's life is headed, or mine, or where our family path might lead next. And yet I know the day of the shark will never be forgotten. Like any mother, I wish, I pray, and I hope that Jonathan and his brothers, Michael and Eric, will be guided to achieve their goals and to help others to overcome the challenges in their lives. I hope Jonathan's story about the struggles of a young man and a family who supported him will be a story he can share, to inspire people and to help others.

Our journey together as mother and son has been more amazing than I could ever have imagined. Together we've found unexpected blessings and joy. My hope, my dream, my desire is that Jonathan will take his experience of loving parents and a family who helped him heal, to another level... that he will go out into the world and help others heal. His story has just begun.

How to Avoid a Shark Attack

Jonathan's Advice

Disclaimer:

The ocean is the home of the shark. If you're in the ocean, you're in the shark's territory.

A few reminders:

Sharks live in the ocean. Accept this simple fact. You are an intruder in their world and they may feel threatened or need to defend their territory.

Always be aware of sharks, but don't let fear stop you from enjoying the ocean.

Treat the ocean with respect. The ocean is beautiful, powerful, and fragile.

Think about sharks in advance and be prepared.

The rules:

- Never swim or surf alone. Remember you are more likely to encounter larger creatures in deep open water.
- Avoid places with lots of seals – the shark's favorite food. You might be a victim of mistaken identity.
- Avoid beaches where sharks have attacked people. These may be good places for sharks.
- Don't go out beyond the rest of the crowd where you'll be the easiest target.
- Stay inside the seals. If a seal swims to shore, something might be chasing it.
- Avoid the ocean during "shark season," August through October in Northern California, when currents bring sharks closer to shore.
- Stay out of the water when the ocean seems agitated with debris washing up on the beach, a sign that the water near shore is abundant for feeding.

- Avoid river mouths. Rivers brings debris attracting seals and fish. Sharks follow their food.
- Do not swim or surf near fishing boats, especially if birds are diving for food in the water. These are signs of a plentiful food supply.
- Use a larger surfboard to create the image of a larger, less vulnerable prey. Sharks are worried for their safety too.
- Be attuned to subtle cues from your environment that tell you something's not quite right.
- If a shark attacks, fight back. Keep trying, and never, *ever* give up.

Jonathan's interview for a National Geographic Channel documentary,
"Shark Battleground – The Red Triangle," filmed at Cronkhite
Beach near the Golden Gate Bridge

Mom learns to surf at Waikiki Beach

Jonathan and Grandma at his Future Leaders For Peace Assembly, Dixie School

Another surfing adventure, this time in Maui

Heading out for surfing in Maui

The 3 brothers – Eric, Michael, and Jonathan on a happy day of surfing in the Dominican Republic. The adventure continues...

Acknowledgments

Special thanks to my mother, Mary McClellan, Jonathan's grandmother, for never giving up hope, for her unending faith, continuous prayers, and for reminding us "this is a story that needs to be told."

Thank you to Reed, Jonathan, Michael and Eric for their inspiration and support in so many ways, and for living this story each day with love and humor.

Thank you to Alan Rinzler, Vicky Van Meter, Tricia Fox, and Michael Pritchard for their encouragement and advice. Thank you to John McCosker for helping us appreciate the mysteries and wonders of the white shark. Everlasting thanks to Pat Norton, Dr. Attaran, Dr. Davis, and many others who helped Jonathan at the beach and in the hospital. Thanks to everyone who helped us while Jonathan was recovering.

My gratitude to my family, the McClellan's, the Seymour's, and the Kathrein's, for a lifetime of love and support.

About the Authors:

Jonathan Kathrein is a graduate of UC Berkeley, winner of the *San Francisco Chronicle* Jefferson Award for Service to the Community, and author of *Don't Fear the Shark*, a metaphor for treating others well. www.dontfeartheshark.com. Jonathan is the co-founder of the nonprofit, Future Leaders For Peace, www.flfp.org, and is a motivational speaker. He has appeared on many radio and TV programs, including Dateline NBC, The Discovery Channel, How to Survive, Travel Emergencies, Fox Mornings on Two, View from the Bay, and People of the Year in Germany. He has lectured to classes at UC Berkeley. His interviews have appeared in *Surfer Magazine, BodyBoarding, The San Francisco Chronicle,* and *Sports Illustrated.* Jonathan's interview for "Primal Scream," was the headline program for The Discovery Channel's "Shark Week."

Margaret McClellan Kathrein is a mother of three sons, and an attorney who practiced with a Chicago law firm specializing in Food and Drug Law. She is the author of *Crisis Management* and co-author of *Occupational Health Law.* She has appeared with Jonathan on many television and radio programs. The author and her family reside in Marin County, in the San Francisco Bay Area.

Other Books by this Author:

Don't Fear the Shark, by Jonathan Kathrein

www.ingramcontent.com/pod-product-compliance
Lightning Source LLC
Chambersburg PA
CBHW061403280526
45784CB00001B/356